Helen J. Sanborn

A Winter in Central America and Mexico

Helen J. Sanborn

A Winter in Central America and Mexico

ISBN/EAN: 9783337254148

Printed in Europe, USA, Canada, Australia, Japan

Cover: Foto ©Andreas Hilbeck / pixelio.de

More available books at **www.hansebooks.com**

CENTRAL AMERICA

AND

MEXICO

BY

HELEN J. SANBORN

PREFACE.

THE knights of old journeyed into distant lands to do deeds of chivalry; the knights of to-day, more practical though not less courageous, go searching for the North Pole, for gold, for knowledge, for adventure; but who of them has gone into distant, uncivilized lands in search of coffee? Such was the errand of the two whose wanderings and observations are recorded in this little volume. The journey was undertaken by Mr. James S. Sanborn, of the firm of Chase and Sanborn, of this city, in the interest of the coffee business of that firm. The author went, as narrated in the first chapter, to be a companion to her father, and, as far as a limited knowledge permitted, to speak the Spanish language. On our return home, notes of our travels were published in the *New England Grocer*, for the interest of the trade.

The publication of these in book form has been demanded so widely, by friends and strangers, that — well, here is the book!

Among the scores of books constantly coming into market, the writer feels that this one has no reason for being and no claim for attention, except from the fact that it treats principally of a country and a people as yet but little known, and rarely visited or written about. The narrative is a true, unvarnished tale; and our earnest desire and hope is that it may awaken in those who read a greater interest in, and regard for, that small, remote, almost unknown republic of Guatemala, which we shall always hold in loving remembrance.

H. J. S.

BOSTON, February, 1886.

CONTENTS.

CHAPTER I.
OFF FOR GUATEMALA!

The Outlook — Discouraging Prospect — The Start — In the South — New Orleans — The Mississippi and the Gulf — Sea-sickness — A Sumptuous Repast — In the Caribbean — Our Indian Pilot — Arrival at Balize 7

CHAPTER II.
BALIZE, LIVINGSTON, AND THE CARIBS.

Tropical Luxuriance — Our Hostelry — An After-Dinner Drive — An Odd Cemetery — Business-hours — Livingston — Strange Sights — The Caribs — Carib Folk-lore — Leaves from Carib History — Race-qualities 19

CHAPTER III.
A VOYAGE ON THE RIVERS DULCE AND POLOCHIC.

The "Sweet River" — The "Golfete" — Lake Izabal — Exorbitant Duties — Inconsistency of Officials — Spanish Politeness — The Marimba — The Indian's Idea — In Crooked Ways — A World of Beauty — Bird and Beast — The Land of Mañana 31

CHAPTER XII.

CHARACTER AND CUSTOMS OF THE PEOPLE.

Aztec and Toltec — Condition of the Indians — Picturesque Costumes — Woman in Guatemalan Society — Love-making — Embarrassing Admiration — Gambling and Drinking — A Hopeless Feature of Society — An Unflattering Picture — The Other Side — A Bird's-eye View of History — Recent Events 170

CHAPTER XIII.

GUATEMALA TO PANAMA.

Rich Resources — Need of Railroads — Good-bye to Guatemala — San José — Tremendous Surf — Fleecing — Tossed by the Billows — A Bitter-Sweet Experience — Two Figures — Blissful Ignorance — A "Norther" — The "Peaceful" Ocean 183

CHAPTER XIV.

PANAMA, ASPINWALL, AND THE ISTHMUS.

The Hand of Providence — An Unhealthy Climate — A Wretched Night — Crossing the Isthmus — Colon — Drink and the Fever — Death in the Air — Tempted to Retreat — The Eloquence of Despair — A Fiery Furnace, 196

CHAPTER XV.

VOYAGE IN AN ENGLISH STEAMER.

A Lawless State of Affairs — A Joyful Departure — A Miscellaneous Company — An Odd Little Baby — All Anchored on Deck — A Terrible "Blow" — Warnings of the "Norther" — Two Waifs — "The Flowing Bowl" — Two Sides of the Question — Sherry in the Pudding-Sauce — Eagerness for Land — A Kind and Thoughtful Captain . 207

CHAPTER XVI.
ACROSS THE GULF TO VERA CRUZ.

A Calm and Placid Voyage — Tired of the Sea — Importunate Boatmen — A Queer Old Place — Byron Recalled — A Spanish Cuisine — Street Scenes — Bandits — "The City of the Dead" — An Unwilling Sojourn 221

CHAPTER XVII.
A DAY'S JOURNEY FROM COAST TO CAPITAL.

The Vegetation of All Zones — A Tribute to Mexican Servants — Wild Beauties — Snow-crowned Orizaba — A Vision of Eden — Marvellous Engineering — A Fairy Town — "La Boca del Monte" — A Mexican Caballero — In the Land of Cut-throats — On the Table-lands — Enveloped in Dust and Smoke — Extensive Stock-raising — A Famous Robber Town — A Helping Hand 232

CHAPTER XVIII.
CITY OF MEXICO.

The Praises of Mexico — An Inviting Field for Tourists — Mexican Hotels — A Great Physical Change — A Beautiful Climate — The Venice of the Aztecs — A Splendid Pageant — Aztec Civilization — A Gifted People — Two Peoples Compared — Free from Care — The Power of Time Defied — The Vile "Lepero" — The Kindly "Aguador" 248

CHAPTER XIX.
IN AND ABOUT THE PLAZA.

"Nieve" and Fruit-Drinks — "Pulque" — The Great Cathedral — A Gorgeous Interior — "Driving the Devil Out" — Vengeance upon Judas — The Mexican Passion-Play — A Perfect Picture — Missions in Mexico — The "Calendar Stone" — The Temple of Sacrifice — The National Palace — Petty Merchants — Haggling — Injured Innocence . . 263

CHAPTER XX.

RAMBLES ABOUT THE CITY.

A Touch of Nature — Snail-paced Mexico — An Unweeded Garden — The Beauty of Mexican Women — Artistic Handiwork — The Grand National Museum — The Academy of San Carlos — The National Pawn-Shop — Procrastination — A Song of To-morrow 279

CHAPTER XXI.

EXCURSIONS IN THE SUBURBS.

The Shrine of Guadalupe — "The Tree of the Sad Night" — A Disastrous Retreat — Alvarado's Leap — Joy and Sunshine — Under a Spell — Floating Gardens — Our Last Indian Breakfast — Chapultepec — A Fine Boulevard — A Spanish Castle — A Lovely Valley — A Restful Scene — A Trysting Place 290

CHAPTER XXII.

HOMEWARD BOUND.

Leaving Mexico — Beggars and Peddlers — A Mining District — In the Desert — Crossing the Frontier — The Importance of Spanish — The Melody of Spanish — George Eliot on Spanish — Flexibility of Spanish — Special Uses of Spanish — A Strange Fascination — Reminders of Mexico — Kit Carson's Cabin — A Familiar Face — Home Again — Retrospection 305

A WINTER IN CENTRAL AMERICA AND MEXICO.

CHAPTER I.

OFF FOR GUATEMALA!

"WHY don't you take your daughter Helen with you on your southern trip?"

This question was asked by a friend of the family as we sat chatting together in the library, one evening, about the journey which my father was soon to take through Central America and Mexico.

My father replied, "I should be very glad to take anybody who could speak Spanish."

"Oh, *will* you take me if I will learn Spanish?" I exclaimed, eagerly. "I will learn it before you go, if you will only promise to take me!"

Much to my own surprise the challenge was accepted, and, although fresh from college and longing for a glimpse of foreign lands, I felt a little dismayed, when I had time for deliberation, at the task I had set myself — to learn a language of which I knew not a word, and make all preparations for a long journey in the short space of less than three months which must intervene before our departure. However, of this I breathed not a syllable to any one, but went to work at once.

We found in planning the journey the greatest difficulty, since it was next to impossible to gain any information about the countries we were to visit. It is truly surprising how very little the people of the United States know about Central America. Their knowledge of the North Pole or Africa is more extensive than of this rich portion of their own continent. The reason is obviously its great lack of facilities for travelling, for there are sufficient attractions to lure all classes of people, from the wealthy tourist to the poor boy "seeking his fortune." There is fine scenery for the traveller; rich mines, valuable woods, and tropical fruits for the speculator; rare plants, birds and animals for the naturalist; wonderful ruins for the antiquarian, and a curious and interesting people for all. But these can be reached only by toilsome journeys on mule-back, and by a most decided experience of "roughing it," so that the country has hitherto been visited almost exclusively by seekers after wealth, adventure, or scientific knowledge, and by only a few of these.

Before we left home we found one or two persons who had been in Central America, and they gave us a most discouraging account of the hardships to be endured in that uncivilized country, where nearly all the inhabitants are Indians, and most of the travelling must be done in the saddle. One gentleman in particular declared that it was utterly unreasonable for a lady to attempt such a journey, and his judgment was corroborated by letters received from American consuls at different points, who, after explaining the dangers and difficulties to be encountered, always added as advice to my father, " *You* can probably take the journey very well, but we would strongly advise you *not* to bring *your daughter.*" However, we were not to be daunted. I felt very sure that I could go wherever my father could; and besides we did not believe more than half that was told us, although on our return we were ready to declare that the most highly colored accounts were no exaggeration.

The largest and most important State of Central America is Guatemala, and the pleasantest and most common route is to go by the Pacific Mail steamer from New York to the Isthmus of Panama, cross the Isthmus by rail and take the Pacific Mail on the other side to San José, in Guatemala, whence there is a railroad to Guatemala City, the capital. The other route is to sail from New Orleans to Livingston, in Guatemala, and cross the country on mule-back to Guatemala City. In this journey both routes were combined, as giving more variety and wider acquaintance with the country. We entered the country by the latter and left it by the former and more common route.

We left Boston on a cold winter day from the New York and New England depot, by the Virginia Midland route, passing through New York, Philadelphia, Baltimore, Washington, Richmond, Charlotte, Atlanta, and Mobile, to New Orleans. We spent a day each in Baltimore and Richmond, where we were most pleasantly entertained by friends; but aside from this the journey through the Southern States was uninteresting. From the car windows one sees for the most part long stretches of rather barren fields and wretched negro huts, the monotony being broken only at the stations, where crowds of negroes are always hanging about, shouting and laughing. In many of the cities, however, building is constantly going on, business is brisk, and decided progress is shown in mercantile enterprises. With the people of the South we were most favorably impressed. We found them exceptionally social, warm-hearted, and obliging, and all the officials most kind and courteous, far exceeding Northern people in this respect.

One hears about the war on every hand. Conversation is full of "before the war," "during the war," and "since the war." The following story admirably illustrates this point: —

It is said that Oscar Wilde, in his visit to the South, took a moonlight walk with a young lady, to whom he made the not very original but entirely sincere remark, —

"How beautiful the moonlight is! The moon never looked lovelier than it does to-night!"

To which the young lady replied with emphasis, "Oh, Mr. Wilde, you ought to have seen that moon 'before the war'!"

In New Orleans we found the exposition in progress, but left it for our return trip, as we had but two days before the sailing of the steamer for Central America. We were mainly impressed with New Orleans as a very dirty city, having a climate rivaling that of New England, for the first day we were there was as mild as spring, and the second as cold as midwinter in Boston.

The morning of our departure, on our way to the wharf, we were driven through most wretched streets, which gave no evidence of being repaired since the foundation of the city. They were full of ruts and mud-holes, which caused the coach to bang about in an alarming manner. In addition, we ran into a mule team, driven by a negro, who protested to our driver calmly but persuasively, "If yo' kill dis mule, it'll cost yer mor'n dat load'll fetch yer." The threat was telling, and we were finally extricated and landed at the wharf alive, but well shaken up.

The steamer *Wanderer*, on which we embarked, is a small steamer, of only 531 tons, and has poor accommodations for passengers, there being no saloon or promenade deck, and hardly space enough for a chair between the staterooms and railing.

There was a goodly number of passengers on board, many of them attracted to Central America by the railroad projected by President Barrios to be built from the coast to the capital. There were but two ladies — how thankful I was that there were two, for I had feared there would be none — and with them and their husbands we became well acquainted and passed many pleasant hours. The two gentlemen were Scotch — one living in Montreal, and the other in British Honduras.

For the first afternoon and evening we were on the Mississippi, and the boat moved as quietly as if on a pond. We saw the sugar plantations, rice fields, and levees, and had a glorious sunset. By half-past nine that evening the steamer had crossed the bar, and, as one of the Scotchmen said, began "to rock a wee bit." The next morning she was fairly out in the Gulf, tossing and pitching in a "chop sea," and everybody was sea-sick. One gentleman declared "the steamer could jump sixty different ways a minute, and perform more antics than an acrobat." In the Gulf of Mexico she found ample scope for her powers, for, as the old black stewardess said, "There's the devil in it sometimes." It is a most treacherous body of water; at times as quiet and peaceful as a lake, and then again as raging and tumultuous as a maelstrom. For a few hours we would sit quietly on deck, the water as smooth as glass; then, suddenly, without warning, we would be driven into our rooms by a shower of rain and a fearful tossing of the vessel.

Nearly everybody on board was sea-sick for two days. My case was not one of the most serious, as I never for a moment longed to die or be thrown overboard, as I have been told is the experience of those severely afflicted. As soon as I could I crawled out and sat in a chair by my stateroom door. Then I began to wonder why my father was so quiet and did not appear at all to wish me "good morning" or see how I was. Just then I saw the steward carrying a little tray of tea and toast to him, and learned on inquiry, much to my surprise, that my father was a victim too.

With no one to talk to I had no entertainment save that furnished by my fellow-passengers, and, although far from comfortable myself, was greatly amused by some of their experiences. In the adjoining stateroom was one poor fellow who was terribly sick, and his friends, who were suffering somewhat less, tried very hard to extend their sympathy by occasionally appearing at the door and inquiring, "How are you now, Charlie?" But this question, jerked out with great speed and vehemence, was the extent of their condolence, for they could never wait for an answer, but with the greatest eagerness hastened to avail themselves of the neighboring rail, that most valuable and popular resort at such times.

On the afternoon of the second day we had all sufficiently recovered to sit on deck, and think about having a little supper brought to us. How we discussed that supper beforehand! A bride never gave more careful thought to her trousseau than our party of six to that meal; for, although we had been fasting for a long time, we were not yet suffering the pangs of real hunger, and were greatly in doubt as to just what would meet the demands of the case. After much debate we presented the steward with the following order:—

Mr. P. — Potatoes and salt beef.
Mrs. P. — Crackers and cheese.
Mr. A. — Salt fish and boiled potatoes.
Mrs. A. — Ice, celery, and salt!
Mr. S. — Tea.
Miss S. — Sardines.

Our anxious thought had not been in vain; the meal was a perfect success, and we felt as if we had had a banquet.

The fourth day we were in the Caribbean sea, and had a little respite from rocking. It was a beautiful day. The water was smooth and of a delicate sea-green color; flying fish and sea-cranes were all about the vessel, and the peninsula of Yucatan was in sight. It is a desolate, uninhabited shore, with the wreck of a vessel visible, and an old ruined castle of stone, which has been there hundreds of years, but has long been tenanted only by sea-birds, which flock there in thousands. We passed one fishing vessel, and saw in the distance a steamer with all sails set. These were the only ships seen on the voyage, and Yucatan was the only point of land.

After our calm day we hoped for a peaceful night's rest, but the wind blew a perfect hurricane all night, and the steamer creaked and snapped as if it were coming to pieces. Moreover, the machinery was out of order, and frequent stops were made to take soundings. This unpleasant state of affairs continued until the afternoon of the fifth day, when we were nearing Balize, and were in calmer waters.

The sea all about here is full of dangerous coral reefs, and wrecks, which are very frequent, are hailed with delight by the natives, who gladly plunder the lost vessel. As evening came on we saw many lights marking these numerous reefs, and at 10 o'clock were opposite the "English Key," where an Indian pilot was to come on board. The captain whistled, and a small sail-boat appeared and came alongside. There were two Indians in the little boat, who seemed entirely overcome by the risk of their situation, and shouted to each other in most nervous, alarmed, and anxious tones while their boat was coming into position and the pilot was getting on board. The captain remarked, "These fellows haven't a bit of nerve; they fly all to pieces at the least excitement."

The pilot was a short, squat Carib Indian, and everything — ship, lives, and cargo — was intrusted to his hands. It was a bright starlight night. Everybody was on deck and perfectly quiet. The Indian, the wheelman, ship's pilot, and captain, all watched from the pilot-house, looking out upon the reefs toward the lights of Balize. The silence was broken only by the Carib's orders, given every few minutes. The steamer barely crept along, taking a crooked path, picking its way among the dangerous reefs. At last, at the end of two hours, just at midnight, the anchor dropped, and the gun proclaimed to Balize that the *Wanderer* had come.

CHAPTER II.

BALIZE, LIVINGSTON, AND THE CARIBS.

THERE being no wharf at Balize, the steamer was obliged to anchor half a mile out, and wait for morning to land passengers, who go ashore in small sailboats that come out from Balize. Early in the morning we were awakened by a babel of strange voices, in which only frequent cries of "Alick!" "Alick!" could be distinguished, and, on looking out, we found the steamer completely thronged with negro boys on the alert for passengers. "Alick" was an active colored boy of some fifteen years, and seemed to be the leader of this numerous crowd. He had a good-sized sailboat, which he managed with the help of another boy, and we engaged him to take us across. The water was full of sharks, great ugly fellows, who completely surrounded the vessel, eagerly snapping at the food thrown out by the steward, and furnishing amusement for the colored boys, who were trying to shoot them with their old muskets. We naturally inquired into the ferocity of these sharks, as we were crossing in the sailboat, and were regaled with stories of men who had been tipped over and immediately devoured, or only escaped by leaving behind an arm or leg. But, besides sharks, these waters abound in very fine fish, and, on inquiring what was the best, "Alick" replied, "Wall, for my eating, give me Jew fish," and we found no one to dispute his taste.

From the sailboat we stepped directly into the yard of the International Hotel, and into the midst of tropical verdure. My father said at once, "How natural it looks, so like the West Indies!" But I had never been in the tropics before, and could only stand spellbound, lost in wonder at so new and strange a scene. There were most beautiful flowers, cocoanut, banana, bread-fruit and mango trees everywhere, but turkey buzzards, lizards, and spiders, as well. To be sure, I had seen pictures of tropical plants, and single specimens in hothouses; but that, after all, gave me a very slight idea of the reality, and I felt as if I had suddenly been transplanted to another world, and could not realize that less than two weeks before I had been in snowbound New England, which was at that moment still wrapt in a mantle of snow.

The hotel was a quite large white building, with broad piazzas on each floor, and made very open, so as to catch all the breezes. The landlord, a Scotchman, was kind, obliging, and entertaining, the very embodiment of chain-lightning in speech and motion, but little can be said in praise of the hotel. The beds were as hard as if constructed entirely of the native mahogany, and the table offered nothing but a very pretentious bill of fare, with no substantial equivalent. Still, one who has travelled in the tropics knows this to be characteristic, and refrains from complaining. However, one circumstance was rather trying — we asked for some lime lemonade, and, because there were "no limes in the hotel," actually had to go without it, when there were bushels of limes within a stone's throw almost to be had for the asking.

Balize is the capital of British Honduras, and a very old town, first settled in 1670, but never entirely free from trouble with the Spanish until

1783. The population is about five thousand, of which three hundred are whites, mostly Scotch, and the rest mainly negroes. The climate is warm, but considered healthy, the excessive heat being tempered by an east wind, which blows nine months out of the year. It is an important depot of British supplies, having a good position on the sea, and at the mouth of a navigable river, and exports tropical fruits, dyewoods, sarsaparilla, and mahogany.

A drive of an hour after dinner showed us the whole place. The main street, which has but few branches, runs parallel with the sea, crossing the river by a bridge which is the great meeting-place of the people, and thronged morning and night by crowds of men and women. The better houses are all white wooden structures, but the negro huts are often most dilapidated, and just ready to tumble down. For a place of its size, there are many public buildings, a hospital, poorhouse, and insane-asylum, supported by the government, numerous schools and churches of various denominations. The natives are very constant attendants at church. Just opposite the hotel was a High Episcopal Church, which holds service three times a day nearly every day in the week, and, when we were there, though it was a week day, was filled to overflowing at its third service. This extraordinary attendance would doubtless be modified somewhat if there were a theatre or any place of amusement there.

The cemetery is very odd looking, the dead being buried in brick vaults above the ground, from the fact that Balize is below the level of the sea. Burial takes place immediately after death, on account of the heat, and a little quicklime is put in each coffin, so that everything soon disappears, and the vaults can be cleaned out every seven years. The barracks are situated just outside the town, in a rather pretty spot by the sea. Here places are arranged for bathing, all fenced in to keep out the sharks, which come and stick their heads through the opening when one ventures to bathe.

The standing army consists of fifty men, all negroes! They are very proud to be called "British subjects," and will "sell their heads" for the honor of that title.

The place is well governed, and the negroes are, for the most part, quiet and peaceable. The laws are very strict in regard to the observance of the Sabbath and the sale of liquors. Licenses are granted, but no saloon is open Sunday, or after eight o'clock at night. This was the only place in all the journey, outside of the United States, where Sunday was observed at all.

On account of the heat, nearly all business is done in the early part of the day. Meals are as follows: Coffee and bread, 5:30; breakfast, 9:30; dinner, 4:30. Ladies seldom go out between breakfast and dinner. By seven o'clock in the morning the market is quite deserted, as all fish and meat have to be disposed of as soon as possible. Fish is caught at two or three o'clock in the morning, and all meat bought Saturday for Sunday has to be parboiled and pickled. The market and all stores are closed at four in the afternoon, after which no one pretends to work.

On the whole, Balize is a rather pretty place, and quite a centre of society and fashion, bearing much the same relation to this part of the country that Boston does to New England.

The next afternoon we embarked once more, and in the morning were off Livingston, where we gladly left the *Wanderer;* although we were sorry to part with the friends we had made, and felt very grateful to the officers and crew, who had, by every kindness and courtesy, atoned in a great measure for the deficiencies of the steamer, and had done all in their power to make the voyage as pleasant as possible.

Livingston is a port of Guatemala, at the mouth of the Rio Dulce (sweet river). It is a settlement of Carib Indians, there being only about twenty or thirty white people. It has a beautiful situation, and looks very pretty from the water. The land rises abruptly from the sea, curving in and out, and is everywhere covered with flowering plants and cocoanut trees. A steep path from the wharf leads up into the town, nearly all of which is visible from the water, and consists mainly of mud huts with thatched roofs. Here "The Boston Tropical Fruit Company" has a warehouse and a small steamer; their secretary lives here, and their plantations are a few miles distant. We found it exceedingly warm, and cared to stay on shore only a few minutes. The American consul, to whom we had letters of introduction, was ill, but we met the secretary of the Fruit Company, a Boston gentleman, and he gave us valuable information about the country which we were soon to penetrate, and the difficulties of travelling there, of which we were continually hearing more and more. Although we had prepared ourselves as well as possible for the journey, our equipments were still incomplete, for we were told that the country was so uncivilized, and the people lived in so primitive a manner, that in parts of the interior we should find none of the comforts and hardly the necessities of life, and that we must purchase hammocks and blankets if we wanted any place to sleep, and, what seemed queerest of all, must provide ourselves with knives and forks, in order not to be reduced to eating with our fingers.

While my father was making necessary arrangements, I sat on the deck of the steamer, looking at the strange scene before me, this Indian pueblo in the heart of the tropics, and I could scarcely believe that what I beheld was real, so totally different was it from anything I had ever seen. Balize now seemed to me almost like home, this was in comparison so much stranger. When I looked at the flowers and trees, and the beauties that nature had so freely bestowed upon this spot,

I wondered if I were in fairy-land; but then there were no fairies, for the inhabitants of this land dwelt in mud huts and were dark enough to be goblins. I felt like pinching myself to see if I were awake or dreaming, and said to myself, "Who am I?" "Where am I?" "Can this be a part of the same earth on which I dwell?"

Every moment now was bringing us to stranger and stranger sights, and I wondered with something of apprehension as to what lay before us, and how we should fare when we came to penetrate into this land and mingle with this uncivilized people.

The Carib Indians that inhabit Livingston are a very interesting tribe, quite distinct and different from the other tribes of Central America, and worthy of special notice. There is some discussion as to their origin, but they probably sprang from the Arrawaks of the Orinoco, another branch of whom, the Araucanians, were the ancestors of the Peruvian Indians.

The Caribs have a legend in regard to their origin; and this legend, told me by a Hungarian, who himself gathered it from the lips of one of them, is somewhat as follows:—

One of the tribes of the Orinoco lived near a pond which was greatly troubled by a water-sprite, who afflicted the people in various ways. There was a pole to mark the spot where he dwelt, and it was believed that if any one touched this pole he would suffer the greatest harm. But the chief had a beautiful daughter, who was exceedingly bold and determined to defy the sprite's power. Accordingly she stole out one dark night to the pond, seized the pole and gave it a vigorous shaking, when, to the surprise of the half-frightened maiden, who was expecting to see some horrid monster, a beautiful youth appeared and dispelled her fears with words of love. They were afterwards married, and their sons were the origin of the Caribs. These sons inherited the turbulent spirit of the father and the bold adventurous spirit of the mother, and soon migrated to the neighboring islands, where they killed the men and married the women. This accounts for a fact which has greatly puzzled scientists, namely, that the men and women, even to this day, speak a different language, the men when together considering it a deep disgrace to use the language of the women; and if perchance one lets fall a word of the woman's talk, he is greatly jeered at.

At the time of the discovery of America the Caribs were the most important tribe on the coast of South America, and in the islands of the Caribbean Sea, and were the cannibals that Columbus found and described. In the invasion of the Europeans they were very fierce and aggressive, and offered such a long and determined resistance that many of them perished. At St. Vincent, one of their principal islands, a slave-ship was wrecked, and thus they became mingled with negro blood. In 1796 they were so troublesome that the English transported them to Ruatan, on the coast of Honduras, whence they dispersed, one of their chief settlements being in Truxillo of Honduras. Afterward, when a controversy arose as to whether the civil or priestly authority should be supreme, the Caribs, siding with Carrera, the President of Guatemala, who supported the civil party, ran away from Truxillo, and came to Livingston, where they now number about one thousand. They have lost their old fierce and warlike character and are now quiet and peaceable.

They have an olive complexion, round heads, abundant black hair, usually straight, but sometimes kinky; they are short and squat, but strongly built, muscular and very erect. It is only lately that they have worn any clothing, and do so now only under compulsion from the government. The women are often handsome and have a queenly gait; they frequently do the work while the men play the hero. The Caribs are specially noticeable for keeping themselves very distinct, and never intermarrying with other tribes. They have very strong family feeling, which is often troublesome to those who are dependent upon them for labor and supplies. For instance — they will not sell, at any price, their market goods until every Carib has first been supplied. They always work by the task, and will do a certain amount for small pay; but when that task is done, even if it be in the morning, and they have earned but five cents, no amount of money would tempt them to do a stroke more.

CHAPTER III.

A VOYAGE ON THE RIVERS DULCE AND POLOCHIC.

THE steamer on which we embarked at Livingston was one of an excellent line established within the last three years, running up the rivers Dulce and Polochic into the interior of Central America. The owners are enterprising men from the United States, who have had great difficulties to overcome in navigating these shallow, swift-running rivers, formerly traversed only by Indian canoes. The first steamer launched on these waters was lost. The present one — a very commodious steamer, made to draw only about six feet of water — was built on the Pearl River, La., and brought by its adventurous owners away across the Gulf, reaching its haven only through much risk and danger. Before embarking we heard much of the fine scenery before us, and many on the *Wanderer* had said, "I do wish I could take the sail up the river"; still we had no idea of the wonder and beauty we were to behold.

I was much troubled at first when I found I was to be the only lady passenger, but the officers and all on board did everything to make my position as pleasant as possible.

We started in the afternoon up the Rio Dulce, and an enchanting view lay before us for several hours. There has been no surveying in this part of the country, so it is impossible to give exact measurements, but for at least ten miles the river runs through a cañon, which is a wonderful curiosity, like our western cañons, but far more beautiful, because instead of barren walls of rock is most luxuriant tropical verdure. The stream is very narrow and the banks rise exactly perpendicular from the water hundreds of feet, covered with a perfect tangle of tropical trees, shrubs, and climbing vines, making two emerald walls of indescribable loveliness. Occasionally a limestone rock crops out, assuming fantastic forms, once like an old Spanish fortification and again forming "las tiendas," an exact imitation of the stores of this country, even to the barred doors and windows, which were perfectly represented by leafless vines stretching across portions of the rock. The river is very winding, and every turn reveals new beauties. Once it makes a perfect elbow, called "The Maiden's Turn," and often bends so sharply that there is no passage visible. To enhance still further the enjoyment of this scene, we were sailing under the blue sky of the tropics and in the midst of such peace and quiet as are found in the haunt of nature only. The puffing of the steamer, and our own voices were the only sounds to be heard, and an occasional Indian canoe gliding noiselessly by, or the flight of some startled bird, were the only signs of life.

Leaving the cañon the river suddenly broadens out into the "Golfete," three or four miles wide and about fifteen miles long. Fair islands dot the surface, but only one is inhabited, and there are no signs of habitation on the shores. On either side is a range of mountains, branches of the Andes, and these beautiful and majestic forms, covered with lasting verdure, dotted with fleecy clouds, like little villages, and ever changing in color and appearance, were from this time until we left the country our constant companions, ever growing nearer and nearer, until at last we painfully climbed on mule-back to their very summits.

At the end of the "Golfete" begins Lake Izabal, and here, on a picturesque point, are a few Indian huts, and the remains of an old Spanish fort, "San Felipe," built long ago to ward off the ravages of pirates. There is a farce of a customhouse here, and we were obliged to stop for a little boat, containing three natives, to come out and examine the ship's papers. This assumption of authority on the part of such ignorant and uncivilized beings seemed very laughable, but they doubtless thought in those few instants of time they had exercised great power and covered themselves with glory. Unused as yet to the country and the natives, we foolishly asked, "What do the people do here?" and the answer was, "Nothing; they lie in the sun and dream away their lives."

Lake Izabal is a beautiful sheet of water, twelve miles broad and thirty-six miles long, one of the largest lakes in Guatemala. It was calm and peaceful that afternoon, but the captain told us it was often wrought into fury by winds from the mountains, and became both tumultuous and dangerous.

About two-thirds up the lake is the pueblo of Izabal, composed, of course, of mud huts, and having a population of about six hundred. The captain, a young man, recently married, lives here with his wife, and they and a few relatives constitute the white population. Like most of these Indian villages it has a beautiful situation, for the Indian is a true lover of nature, and never fails to select the fairest spot he can find for his home.

In the time of Cortes it was renowned as a pottery market and is so still, the Indians who go on pilgrimages to Esquipulas coming here to sell their pottery. It is also one of the chief ports of Central America, and the seat of the custom-house, Livingston being a free port. This custom-house is conducted on very peculiar principles, the officers being natives, very ignorant and often unreasonable. Three of them, dark, barefooted, unintelligent looking fellows, came on board, fairly grinning in their authority, enough to make any one rebellious at the thought of having such men go through his baggage. Duties are levied according to weight, which makes some charges very exorbitant. A German in Guatemala told us it cost him over $200 to get a cooking-stove through, an article entirely unknown in this country. Powder and firearms are regarded with the greatest suspicion, on account of the frequent insurrections, and the duty on a common pistol is $6.00. A young man on board our steamer, a native of the country, just returning from a visit to the United States, had to pay $22.00 on a few little articles, such as pictures and ordinary looking-glasses, a great deal more than they had cost him. The officers are also very particular that the goods correspond exactly to the written statement, and if there is the least difference the whole is confiscated. A merchant in the interior lost a box of paint brushes because there were four or five less in the box than was stated in the inventory. Moreover these officers are as inconsistent as they are unreasonable, sometimes performing their duty with the utmost rigidity, and at other times, if they happen to feel lazy or good-natured, letting almost anything pass. This happened to be the case with our baggage, which they did not examine at all; luckily for us, perhaps, for according to their other caprices we should have had to pay about a thousand dollars, our equipments for the journey into the interior being extensive.

We spent all day Sunday at Izabal, and, although it was very warm, went on shore to see the place, a thing which was soon accomplished. In the morning the fife and drum called out the whole town in review, for every man is a soldier. The barracks were in the prettiest spot, at a little rising in the back of the town, but the army, consisting of dark, ragged, and barefooted men, was far from formidable. The hotel was the usual mud hut with one room, but the landlord had the manners of a titled lord, and received us with a great show of politeness, saying, in Spanish, "My house is yours, gentlemen." That being the case, we thought we would test his unbounded generosity with a request for some lemonade, the ingredients of which — limes, sugar, and water — were almost as cheap there as mud. Four glasses were duly prepared, and the landlord was presented with a dollar, which he calmly pocketed, returning no change. Evidently, if the house was ours, the lemonade was his, and we felt a little disgusted with our first lesson in Spanish politeness. This is often the effect on Americans, who fail to appreciate such etiquette. An amusing story is told of a Yankee who proceeded to ride off with a very valuable horse, after the owner had said, "That horse is yours, sir," and was only stopped by greatest entreaties on the part of the owner, who was ever after very careful about being polite to Americans.

That evening we heard for the first time the national instrument, or "marimba," composed of strips of wood of different lengths, from which hollow tubes of wood are suspended, the whole being mounted on legs and played by three men, who strike it with little sticks. The music is very sweet, sounding like a stringed instrument with something the depth of a drum. It sounded exceedingly beautiful that night as the strains floated across the lake to our steamer.

At Izabal we parted with some of the passengers, but the most interesting remained: one of the owners of the line, who proved an invaluable friend all the time we were in Guatemala; an elderly man, a Hungarian by birth, who gave me much information about the country; the son of a Boston clergyman; and a young "Guatemaltecan," who afterward proved of the greatest assistance to us in our overland journey.

A sail of an afternoon brought us to the mouth of the Polochic, and into "the wilds of Central America." It was a lonely, swampy place, with swarms of mosquitoes, myriads of green parrots, and monkeys, and baboons, that shrieked and howled as loud and strong as so many lions. Here we had to change steamers, and wait for morning, because it is not possible to navigate the Polochic in the night. The steamer to which we were to change awaited our arrival, guarded by a single lone watchman, the only human being within fifty miles. This steamer was smaller than the other one, but equally pretty, and was made flat-bottomed, to draw as little water as possible. It was the first steamer ever built in Guatemala, and of course a great wonder to the Indians, who used to come in crowds to see it. A description given by one of them to a companion may be interesting: "It is bigger than two churches put together, and has a big kettle in it always boiling. The man makes it 'toot, toot,' it wags its tail, and off it goes faster than an Indian can trot."

We started early next morning, and had a beautiful sail all day. The Polochic proved to be a very curious river, a winding mountain-stream, very shallow, full of snags and ever-changing sandbars, and with a swift current, making it very difficult of navigation. Then, in addition, it is the most crooked stream in the world, always curving, and winding, and turning upon itself, sometimes making actual double bow-knots. These windings make it the more interesting, and often we were to all appearances in a very small pond, completely hemmed in by mountains before and behind, with no possible exit visible. The turns are in many cases so abrupt that the steamer actually touched the bank, and had to be pushed off by poles, the men being all prepared, and acting just at the right moment to prevent its getting aground. What is still more remarkable, it is possible to sail for an hour or more, and make only a few feet real progress in the onward direction. We once looked through a little bower made by the vines, and actually saw right beside us a portion of the river on which we had sailed an hour before. A certain lady, when asked her opinion of the Polochic, replied, "When the crooked ways are made straight, I think there will be a great deal of work to be done on the Polochic."

The land all about was low and moist, and teeming with vegetable and animal life. There were many valuable woods, as mahogany, and many curious trees; the "ceiba," distinguished among all others by size and appearance, being in shape a mushroom with branches at right angles; a locust without branches to the height of seventy or eighty feet; and a tree called "pacaya," bearing nuts in a cluster, like grapes. There was a great profusion of vines, at least twenty varieties, many of which were covered with beautiful flowers, filling the air with fragrance. Some were like our morning-glory, but open all day, and of all shades of color; some were trumpet-shaped, and of a bright red color; others were like our cultivated arbutulum, but far larger and richer. The vines twined themselves over every dead stump and old tree, transforming them into beautiful bowers, Corinthian columns, or arches of delicate green.

There were many rare birds: cranes, black and white; the "Quaca Mayor," with a brilliant red breast; a beautiful blue kingfisher, who always gave to his fellows the warning signal of our approach; exquisite humming-birds, of which there are thirty-six varieties; and flocks of green parrots, flying through the air with loud chattering. Monkeys and baboons were visible in the trees, and on the banks and sandbars were numbers of hideous alligators quietly sunning themselves, until aware of our approach, when with one plunge they disappeared in the water. Lizards of every variety and color, including iguanas, were abundant. The latter are loathsome looking creatures, clothed in scales like an alligator, with a long tail, a pouch under the throat, and spines along the back. They are sometimes five feet long, and of different colors, green, yellow, and fox-color, though usually hard to distinguish from the branches of the trees to which they cling. They live on vegetable food, the mangrove tree being their favorite, but they have a hole in the ground, to which they retire in the wet season. The eggs and flesh are greatly prized for food, the meat being white and tender, and much like chicken.

At 4 P. M. we reached the head of navigation, and the wretched Indian village of Panzos, which was hot, damp, and swarming with mosquitoes and sand-flies, very tiny creatures, whose bite is far worse than that of the mosquito.

There were only two persons here who spoke

English, the agent of the line and his wife, a young couple who were the picture of contentment in this miserable place, where several families before them had been unable to live.

The hotel was a mud hut of one room, but, fortunately for us, the steamer was obliged to wait for a load of coffee from the interior, and we most thankfully accepted the captain's invitation to remain on board.

From Panzos we were to start on our trip across the country to Guatemala City, and, having previously learned that we could not obtain even a mule at Panzos, had taken the precaution to telegraph from Izabal into the interior for a carriage if it could be obtained, or, if not, for mules, and we had hoped to find them, with a guide, awaiting us. They had not come, of course, and with a longer experience in the country we should not have expected it, for we were now in the land of mañana (to-morrow), and, whether patiently or impatiently, wait we must.

CHAPTER IV.

LIFE AMONG THE INDIANS.

The Indians with whom we were now to eat, sleep, and travel, are entirely different from those of North America, being a peaceable, honest, docile, and cleanly race; not a warlike, but an agricultural people; not nomadic, but living in villages; not savage, but semi-civilized; tilling the soil, weaving cloth, making pottery and building houses. They are of a brown or copper color, with black hair and eyes, low foreheads, but without the prominent cheek-bones, and with kind, pleasant, and often handsome faces. They are noticeably small, being below medium height, squarely built, and with small hands and feet. They are so honest and peaceable that Central America is the safest place in the world in which to travel, and altogether to an American, with our idea of the Indian as a painted savage, they are quite an attractive people. But the poor things are the "beasts of burden" of the country, pack mules being so rare that almost everything is transported on Indian backs, the amount they carry being wonderful. The burden is placed in a wooden cage or basket, to which a strap is attached and passed around the head, so that the weight comes upon the forehead. In this manner, with a weight of over a hundred pounds, they trot off at a queer but rapid pace, making twenty and twenty-five miles daily, and for this arduous work they are never paid more than a "real" (twelve and one-half cents) a day. Much of the coffee is brought in this way from the interior down to the ports; thousands of dollars are entrusted to them, the merchant simply saying, "Your cargo is money," and not one dollar was ever lost or stolen.

One of the most peculiar characteristics of the Indians is their silence and stolidity in the presence of the white man, though, when not aware of his presence, they will talk and laugh uproariously, and are really a very social race, always going in companies in their travels. They are very proud, and guard themselves most carefully against any expression of surprise, admiration, or wonder. We had an excellent example of this while at Panzos, in observing a party of Indians who had just come down from the country, and had never seen the steamer before. They all came down to the bank, and gazed at it earnestly and carefully for at least fifteen minutes, evidently "taking it all in," but never exchanging a word with one another, or allowing their faces to express the slightest emotion, though they must have been overwhelmed with astonishment at so strange and stupendous an object.

These Indians constitute five eighths of the population of Guatemala, the rest being mainly "ladinos," of mixed Spanish and Indian blood, there being comparatively few descended directly from the old Spaniards; even President Barrios himself had a dash of Indian blood in his veins. The poorer classes of these "ladinos" are little if any superior to the Indians, and often lazier and dirtier. They always speak Spanish, while the Indians retain their own language.

On the evening of the second day in Panzos we were rejoiced to hear that the carriage had come, and walked up the road to inspect it. It was the only carriage between here and Guatemala, a distance of over two hundred miles, and had formerly been used on the Pacific side, until the railroad drove its owner with his coffee wagons and mules into the interior. This carriage had to be taken all to pieces and transported on Indians' backs across the mountains, a distance of over a hundred miles, whence the road was wide enough for it to be used. It was a large, strong, two-seated, covered vehicle, resembling a beach wagon, but furnished with a strong iron brake for the mountains, and completely covered with mud inside and out; nevertheless, the captain assured us that in this "turn-out" we should be travelling "in style." It was drawn by two stout mules, and the driver was a young "ladino," a happy-go-lucky, rather capable fellow, wearing clothes of an odd coarse cloth, with a bright red scarf about his waist, which gave him rather a jaunty appearance.

We arranged with him to start at five o'clock sharp in the morning, so as to avoid travelling in the heat of the day, and I fought mosquitoes more cheerfully that night than usual, because it was the last. Next morning we were ready at the appointed time, but six o'clock came and seven, still no carriage appeared. Finally, about eight the boy drove up; not at all abashed by his tardiness, for, like the rest of the people in this country, he was probably never "on time" in his life, and never expected to be. On being questioned, he said "Dolly" (one of the mules) got away in the night, and he had been hunting for her several hours. It was no use scolding, and we started off as cheerfully as possible, but we had not gone two rods before we stopped, and the boy got out and began to tie up a broken whiffletree, which from all appearance had been half-broken several days, but which he would never have thought of mending until we got started and it gave out entirely, even if he had been in Panzos a week with nothing else to do.

Very soon I ventured to address a few words in Spanish to the driver, for I knew the time had come when I must do all the talking, and we should be in a sorry plight if I failed. To my joy, he understood me, and I understood his answer. He did not speak a very clear or grammatical Spanish; and if mine sounded odd to him he was too polite to betray it by the slightest expression, and treated my attempt as if he thought I had spoken Spanish all my life. After a few hours we got accustomed to each other so we could talk very well: I could ask all that was necessary; and if at any time I did not understand, he would take the greatest pains to explain to me until I did.

In a short time we were out of Panzos and jouncing up and down over a terrible road. It was considered to be in a pretty good condition, as this was the dry season; but the worst American country road, in the spring, multiplied by one hundred, would be only an approximation to this road that first day. There were great mudholes into which one wheel would disappear entirely, while the other was elevated several feet in the air, and as a consequence one of us was almost landed on the ground while the other savagely grasped the side of the carriage, and tried to hang suspended from above. Considering that one of us weighed 260 pounds and the other only 140, the seriousness of the situation when the " fat man's " side tipped up may be fully appreciated. What prevented the wagon from tipping over is a mystery, but the boy assured us it *could* not upset; and there must have been something in the construction which rendered it a physical impossibility, for there was every opportunity for performing this feat. Many times we got out and walked; many times we were stuck in bogs where it seemed as if we could not possibly advance; but the mules were brave and stout; and summoning all their energies, would draw us out safely and neatly, where four horses would have failed utterly. "Cassimir," the driver, did his part well, and worked nearly as hard as the mules, shouting and urging them on. His Spanish jargon so amused us that we sat and laughed even in the most perilous places. It was something after this fashion, as near as it can be reproduced: "*Hyba mula, hyba soldar, hyba colleela, hyba!*" When very much excited and in a most difficult spot, he would stand up, use the whip vigorously, and shout at the top of his voice, "*Hydja, cerca, soldar holda colleela!*" which, with the addition of much crowing and screaming, and calling of "Dolly" and "Selosa" (the names of the mules), was exceedingly funny, and diverted us for several days.

We reached our first stopping-place, excepting mud-holes, about noon — a place called "Teleman," which consisted of a few mud huts. As we drove up, the young "Guatemaltecan" who had been with us on the steamer came out to meet us with his hands full of fruit, and his "sweet oranges" in English was a welcome sound. As he proved to be an invaluable friend to us in the journey, and as he illustrates the character of the best class among the natives, he is worthy of special notice. He was a youth of twenty-one or two, of medium height and slender, with the usual complexion of the country, very black hair and eyes, and a very dark skin, but was, on the whole, rather fine looking. He bore a Spanish name, and his dress and manners were those of a polished gentleman. He belonged to one of the first families, his father being secretary to the "jefe" (Governor) of one of the principal districts of Guatemala. He had been in the United States three months, where he had learned a little English, and was now returning home to one of the interior towns, having had to wait in Panzos for his own horse to be sent him. He had travelled with us all the way from New Orleans, but we had spoken with him only once or twice, as he knew but little English and was very bashful and retiring, so that we were surprised as well as much pleased when he awaited us here and signified his purpose to accompany us, and serve us in our journey.

After a short rest at Teleman we went on again, in the same see-saw fashion, the young man going in advance to have dinner ready for us when we should arrive at the next place, we having so far subsisted on a lunch from the steamer. All the time we were surrounded by a beautiful tropical growth, but our unexpected and intermittent risings and fallings rather interfered with our enjoyment of the scenery. In about the middle of the afternoon we came upon a great tree lying right across the road; and at the sight our hearts sank within us, for the road all the way had been narrow, with an embankment on one side and thick woods on the other, so we thought we were completely blockaded twenty miles from a hut or Indian. Under these trying circumstances what did that driver do but sit back in the wagon and laugh as hard as he could. Not being of his careless disposition, and failing to see any joke about it, we hastily made investigations, and to our own surprise found a path at the side of the road, among the trees, through which the carriage was just able to pass; and fortunate enough it was, for there was not another spot for miles where this would have been possible.

Without further mishaps we reached "La Tinta," at seven o'clock in the evening, and found a wretched place, one of the worst of these miserable Indian towns, without even the usual mud hotel of one room. Arriving there in the dark, in a place so unknown, amidst a strange people, with peculiar customs and a foreign language, we felt when we got out of the carriage like two lost and bewildered waifs, knowing not what to do or which way to turn. But our young friend soon appeared and relieved us of further anxiety. He led the way to the "cabildo," a government building found in every town, a free stopping-place for all the Indians travelling with burdens. It corresponds somewhat to our City Hall, and is the headquarters of the "comandante," a government official who has all the Indians under his control. This building was of mud, but whitewashed, and consisted of one room, with the ground for a floor. There was a bench running around the room, a large rough wooden table, on which a candle was burning, and this was all. We learned in a few minutes the force of the oft-repeated Spanish phrase, "no hay" (there is none), for in the whole village there was not a bed, or any article of furniture, no knives and forks, and hardly a dish in which to eat, not a basin of water to bathe our faces, in fact none of what we considered the necessaries of life ; and, worse than all, no English language. What we should have done here without our Spanish friend I am sure I do not know. Our driver was perfectly careless of us and concerned only for his mules. At that time of night no one would have given us anything to eat, we should not have known where to go or what to do, and certainly should have had a most wretched experience had it not been for this young man's kindness. In that miserable mud hut he seemed like a prince, and his words of Spanish like so much magic as he gave orders to one after another, who hastened to do his bidding. In a short time he had dinner before us, having procured fried eggs, "frijoles," "tortillas," and coffee, from a neighboring house, and dishes, knives and forks, and some eatables from his own trunk. "Frijoles," "tortillas," and "café" constitute the living of the Indians, as they never have meat except on feast days. The frijoles are stewed black beans, and taste very much like "Boston baked beans"; the "tortillas" are a coarse cake of the simplest kind. They are made from corn which is ground between two stones, just as it was in Egypt in the time of the Israelites. The corn is then moistened and patted between the hands until a round flat cake is formed, which is baked on a thin sheet of iron over a charcoal fire. These articles of food we had every day for ten days while we were travelling to Guatemala City, and it was exceedingly fortunate that we were not Epicureans.

After dinner, as there was nothing to induce us to sit up but a flickering tallow candle, we swung our hammocks for the night. The "Indians," who were carrying the young man's baggage, and of whom there were several, had already spread their "petates" (straw mats) on the ground, and were asleep just outside the door. Our driver had spread a little piece of blanket right in the dirt in the middle of the road, and was also asleep near the carriage, to which the mules were tied. Almost completely exhausted as we were by our long ride over such a road, our hammocks did not seem like very downy couches, but we slept until about five o'clock, when the Indians roused us preparing for their day's tramp. We were anxious, too, to start, but the boy and one mule were missing and did not appear until between seven and eight o'clock, when he came leading the refractory "Dolly," saying he had been hunting for her since three o'clock. Thereupon it was immediately determined to end "Dolly's" nightly excursions if possible, and two stout lassos were obtained and given to the boy, and after that we had no more trouble of this sort. At last the mules were harnessed, but the boy still lingered; and, when asked the reason, said he "had not taken his coffee," and we saw by his whole attitude that our journey would not begin until after that important event. Everybody here invariably begins his day with a cup of coffee, and the manner of preparation is both peculiar and interesting. The coffee is burned over a charcoal fire until black and bitter, then it is ground and put with water until the whole strength is extracted, and a strong, black tincture of coffee is the result. Enough is made to last a week and it is put on the table every meal, either cold in a bottle, or sometimes heated and brought on in a pot. Only a little is poured into the cup, which is then filled up with hot water, and there is no milk, and rarely sugar, except in the larger towns. At first it tasted very bitter, and we had difficulty in drinking it at all, but after a while got accustomed to it and drank it freely three times a day, as everybody does here. Indeed, in the malarial districts it is said to be most excellent, acting like a tonic, with almost the efficacy of quinine and none of its bad effects.

The second day the road was in a better condition, though gradually ascending. At noon we stopped to rest at a most charming spot, beautiful enough for a fairy's bower. The scene is one of the loveliest among the many pictures which often rise before my mind. On one side was a steep embankment, at the foot of which a mountain torrent roared and foamed over the stones; on the other was a wide opening in the green hillside, through which trickled a little stream, whose banks were covered with most beautiful flowers, delicate mosses and ferns. By the stream an Indian and his wife and baby were sitting, making a picturesque group in their bright colored costumes. They evidently regarded us with much interest, not unmixed with admiration; and, when my father patted the baby on the cheek and put a piece of money into its hand, seemed as delighted as the child, which crowed in great glee. We stopped here only long enough to rest, although I would gladly have lingered, and rose very reluctantly when Cassimir, having finished his nap, signed to us to resume our ride. At night we arrived at a small Indian town, "Tucuru," four thousand feet above the sea, and stopped at a mud hut, the best in the town, and the place where travellers usually stop. The woman of the house was an ugly, rude, disagreeable creature, who was smoking a large cigar and spitting on the floor. But there were several pleasant-looking girls, and one man who was quite agreeable, and who, we found out afterward, was only staying there for a short time, and was "very rich" for this country. We had a better dinner here than usual, there being some fowl in addition to the other fare, and we also had cot beds for the night, though we all slept in the same room with the family.

The cots which were furnished us here, and which we were able to obtain in most of the towns (although often there were not more than three in a whole village), we found preferable to hammocks.

They were most simple in construction, consisting merely of a rude wooden frame with strips of rawhide tacked across, and covered with a straw mat, which was the only bedding. We had to furnish our own blankets for covering, and for a pillow used either a handbag or coat or shawl, though usually the nights were so chilly that we needed all our wraps to keep us comfortable. Of course, on such hard beds, obliged to sleep in all our clothing, we could get very little rest, but we were always so completely exhausted at the end of a day's ride that we could have slept on a stone.

The third day the road was still ascending, and often so steep as to be almost frightful, but commanding fine views, for we were winding in and out among the mountains, and were sometimes on the brink of a steep precipice at the foot of which a little mountain-stream ran, or could look down hundreds of feet and see below us the road on which we had come, while there were still heights above to climb. All the way was bordered by tropical trees and flowers, such as grow in our hothouses, and we had frequent glimpses of tiny waterfalls and cascades, and rockeries covered with delicate mosses and ferns, more beautiful than any garden in America can furnish.

We made our first stop at noon, at Tamaju, five thousand feet above the sea; the usual Indian town, somewhat larger than we had been in before, and the first to boast of a church. Cassimir then informed us, much to our astonishment, that we could go no further that day, for the mules were very tired, in fact Selosa was nearly exhausted, and before us was a great mountain, higher than any we had yet climbed. At the announcement the usual shower of questions which attended every arrival and departure, and in fact was kept up at intervals throughout the whole day, I was obliged to interpret for my father, until I was nearly worn out. "What's the name of the next place?" "How far is it?" "How long will it take to get there?" "What kind of a place is it?" "Are there any beds?" "Is the road bad?" "Can't we go a little farther?" But urging and questioning were vain, the boy was firm, and we had learned from experience to trust to his judgment. One curious thing was observable, he never could tell the distance of one place from another, always in his answer using the words "tal vez" (perhaps), and evidently guessing the distance, sometimes very wildly, but he could always tell, almost to a minute, when we would arrive at a given place, and was very proud of this accomplishment.

We found in the comandante of this place a real gentleman, who received us very cordially, and began at once to make arrangements for our comfort, sending word to his home, near by, for his wife to prepare breakfast, and having cot beds brought into the cabildo for us. It happened, as is the case in towns of any size, that the cabildo consisted of two rooms, one being a jail, and, as this was empty, he politely placed it at our disposal, leaving us a little in doubt at first whether to feel like tramps or honored guests with a spare room.

Our breakfast was ready sooner than usual, for the señora had numbers of Indian girls for servants, all of whom she set at work, and we had, comparatively speaking, a good meal, for there are degrees of difference in tortillas, frijoles, and fried eggs, and besides we had the addition of some meat, which, however, was so tough that we preferred to consider it rather for ornament than use. We were waited on by young Indian maidens, who stole noiselessly in and out like so many dusky phantoms, but ministered to all our wants with ease and grace.

After dinner, in about five minutes, we saw the whole town and paid a visit to the church — like all in the country, a very pretty building externally, but containing hideous, repulsive images, and adorned with tinsel and gewgaws, so as to be scarcely recognized as anything but a pagan church. There was evidence of devotion, however, in the beautiful offerings of fresh flowers before many of the images.

Then our friend left us, for we were now well able to care for ourselves, and there was no need for him to delay longer his journey. To him we shall always feel the deepest gratitude, for he had rendered us most valuable service in a most graceful and modest manner, completely disarming us of all prejudices, and changing entirely our conceptions of the Spanish character. His whole bearing throughout was most admirable. No American, however polished a society gentleman he might be, could have acted in the same capacity under similar circumstances without making himself a "bore."

The quickness of perception and amount of tact that the Spanish possess is truly wonderful, and Emilio Carranza furnishes a good illustration. He understood perfectly the situation, exactly how the country would impress us, and what difficulties it would present; and, without making himself in the least obtrusive or disagreeable, removed all our care and responsibility, and took entire charge of us without seeming to at all. He invariably appeared (sometimes as if from the clouds) at the very moment when we needed him most, did exactly the right thing, and then, without allowing us to thank him, as gracefully withdrew, being careful never to intrude, and only desirous of showing, in the best possible way, the greatest politeness and kindness to strangers in a strange land.

All that was left us with which to beguile the long afternoon was to watch the Indians, a great crowd of whom was gathered about the cabildo. Their costumes, like that of all the Indians throughout the country, was very picturesque. The women's dress consists of a full plaid skirt and a loose, sleeveless waist, embroidered, often elaborately, with the colors of the tribe. The hair, which is long, black, and often beautiful, is sometimes left flowing, but usually wound with a red woollen roll. They are always barefooted, and wear no jewelry except a necklace of beads and money — their necklace being their bank. The dress of the men consists of a loose jacket and trousers of a stout cloth, always white, and, what is remarkable, always clean. We never saw a dirty Indian, and seldom a ragged one. When carrying burdens they wear sandals of leather, and wide hats, and remove their jackets, and roll up their trousers, so as to be as nearly naked as possible. They never wear war-paint or feathers, and the only indication of savageness is the long, cruel-looking "machete," which they always carry, and which is as essential to them as a jack-knife to us, for the woods are so dense with vines and shrubs that they cannot penetrate into them a foot without cutting their way with these long knives.

About the cabildo was a crowd of bright boys, evidently curious to see us, but a little afraid. They would approach in a body as near as they dared, and then with a laugh and shout disappear around the corner of the building. We offered them all the encouragement possible, and each time they ventured nearer until their curiosity was finally satisfied. This merely illustrates with what interest we were everywhere regarded. Always on arriving at a place the driver was questioned long and earnestly in regard to us, and his air of pride and ownership in us was very amusing.

The people were anxious to converse, always showing disappointment when they found one of us could not speak Spanish. They recognized us immediately as Americans, and expressed the greatest admiration for the United States, and a desire to speak English. Our driver learned to say "all right" with perfect understanding of its meaning, and was so proud of it that he constantly displayed this knowledge before the Indians, telling them he could speak English, with such an air as to make them believe he knew the whole English language.

As soon as it was dark, which was directly after sunset, for there is no twilight in the tropics, we repaired to the jail to pass the night; but sleep was long in coming, for a great crowd of Indians just outside the door were talking fast and loud in their queer guttural language. Although we had now been living with the Indians three days, and the fear I first felt (for I had fear at first) had almost entirely vanished by seeing every day their kindly faces, still I must confess to a great deal of nervousness this night there in that lonely hut completely surrounded by Indians. The comandante was in his house, some distance off, our driver asleep on the ground somewhere, we knew not where, and Emilio Carranza, hitherto our protector, miles away. It was really startling to hear these Indians, usually so silent, talking so loudly and earnestly, and I became so frightened that I half believed they were plotting against our lives, and lay there trembling, expecting every moment to see the door burst open and the Indians rush in upon us. I spoke to my father, but I did not tell him I was afraid. Oh no! I would not confess my weakness! But he confessed to a nervousness of quite a different sort, and declared he was all out of patience with such a noise. Just then there came a fresh arrival, and a new voice struck up in a sharp falsetto key which banished all hope of sleep, and so exhausted my father's patience that he called out the forcible

English "Shut up!" in stentorian tones. Immediately all was silence, every voice was hushed, and the talkers vanished as if into thin air, without the sound even of a footstep. I rose from my cot and looked out of the window. The moon was shining brightly; not an Indian was in sight; the quietness and peacefulness of the night soothed my spirit, and I felt how foolish my fears had been.

But even now we could not sleep, for then there came stealing upon the stillness the sounds of the marimba, sweet and monotonous, but not soporific, the same strain repeated over and over. It was a feast day, and the Indians were having a dance somewhere in the village, and played this one tune without an instant's cessation for hours and hours. Finally, about midnight, the sounds died away, and we slept.

CHAPTER V.

A WEEK IN AN INDIAN VILLAGE.

OUR loss of half a day at Tamaju on account of the fatigue of the mules was very discouraging, for we had planned to reach in four days the village of Coban, one of the largest interior towns, where there was a hotel, and, we hoped, some opportunity for rest and comfort. It was also the end of the carriage road, and there we should have to change our mode of travelling, hiring mules for riding, and Indians, or "mozos," as they are always called, to carry our baggage. Our driver gave us little encouragement as to the possibility of reaching Coban in one day more, but we were exceedingly anxious, and urged more strongly than ever the importance of an early start. Quite to our own surprise he actually called us at three o'clock in the morning, having, through a growing affection or a better understanding of our ways, made a great effort to carry out our request. He had his mules all harnessed, and coffee ready, so we set out on our journey at once. The moon was full and high in the heavens, and by its light, which was almost as bright as that of day, we climbed the great mountain until we reached its very top. At eight o'clock we stopped for breakfast at "Taltic," a small but flourishing Indian town all nicely laid out with garden plots, and having an air of thrift we had not seen before, for the Indians all over the town were at work building fences and making gardens. The town was at such an elevation that it seemed very cold. Every Indian wore a great blanket over his shoulders, and we were obliged to wrap ourselves up as warmly as possible. We took breakfast with a pleasant and attractive family, though the hut bore the sign "se vende aguardiente" (brandy is sold here), the brandy of the country, very strong, and disagreeable to any but natives.

Near by was a very pretty church in which services were being held in honor of a feast day, "the feast of candles," and the church was full of Indians kneeling upon the floor and chanting a hymn in Spanish in response to the priest. They sang with sweet voices, but the music was strange and monotonous.

By nine o'clock we began our journey again; the boy assuring us that if we could reach the next village by noon, we should arrive at Coban that night. My duties as interpreter then became exceedingly arduous, for my father seemed to think that our getting to Coban depended upon the number and frequency of my questions to the driver, and at intervals of every fifteen minutes would say, "Ask him how far it is now." How anxious we were all through the hours of that morning, and when we drove into "Santa Cruz" were almost afraid to look at our watches, but, to our joy as well as Cassimir's triumph, the hands pointed to precisely twelve o'clock.

The towns were now growing larger and thriftier, and here there were several coffee plantations, and in the "plaza" a large group of Indian women removing the coffee berry from the pulp, there being no machinery in these small towns. They were sitting on the ground with baskets of the red berries before them, and in their embroidered dresses, with streaming black hair, made a picturesque group. They work very fast, but are paid only six and one fourth cents a day.

After the mules had rested we passed on, and in a few hours saw from the top of a hill a village which, with its white houses and church spires, looked exceedingly pretty.

From the distance it resembled very much a little New England village, and I thought we were at last to see something like home. Completely exhausted as we were with more than a hundred miles of travelling over such a rough road, we hailed with delight our first real halting-place on the way to Guatemala. It was the home of Cassimir and the mules, and they were as happy as we. Though almost too exhausted to speak, we stood up in the carriage and shouted, "Hurrah!" The boy snapped his whip vigorously, crowed, screamed, and shouted in triumph to the mules, "à las cuatro, Coban" (at four o'clock, Coban), and we dashed down the hill and into the village with rejoicing hearts. But, alas, our joy was turned into disappointment when we drove into Coban, and found it the usual Indian town; larger, to be sure, and in many respects better, but nothing like what its distant appearance had deluded us into believing.

We went at once to the hotel, which was kept by a German lady, whose daughters, to our relief, spoke English. I had become so weary with questioning the driver that I declared to my father that whether English was spoken at the hotel or not, he would have to do the talking, for I could not speak another word. "Hotel Aleman," like all the houses in the place, was of whitewashed adobe, a long one-storied building (there was only one two-storied house in the village), containing many rooms, but with stone floors, and, like all adobe houses, dark, damp, and cheerless. But we stayed in the house very little, for there was always bright sunshine out of doors, and in front of the hotel a beautiful garden where roses and violets were in blossom the year round.

The fare we found very good, and we did more than ample justice to every meal. The fact is, we were nearly starved, and must have acted almost as ravenous as the Marchioness at her first banquet with Dick Swiveller. The arrangement of meals in all these countries is very different from ours. They never have breakfast before ten or twelve o'clock; but have on rising a cup of coffee and piece of bread. The bread at this hotel was delicious; not in loaves like ours, but in all sorts of fancy shapes, some kinds resembling cake more than bread. This and the nice fresh cheese they had, we enjoyed very much. Coffee was made after the manner already described, but was carefully prepared and very good. We had, too, the luxury of milk and sugar. One coffee shrub in the garden was sufficient for the supply of the hotel.

We were much interested in the Indian girl, "Candelaria," who was the busiest body in the whole house. She waited on the table, took care of the rooms, brought water for the house in a jar on her head, went to the market, and in fact was doing something every moment and yet never seemed to be tired. Sometimes we heard her grinding coffee at nine o'clock in the evening, and she was always the first one up in the morning.

Coban is called very pretty, although I never could see anything to admire in adobe architecture. Many of the houses are large; every house, whether large or small, and all the fences are kept freshly whitewashed, and the whole place is as neat and clean as possible. It has a fine situation in a fertile valley at an elevation of over four thousand feet, so that the climate is very agreeable and healthful. Although quite warm in the middle of the day, it is always cool in the shade and at morning and evening. To us, coming as we did from the hot coast lands, it seemed very cold, and at first I shivered in my warmest wraps, only convincing myself that it must be warm by looking at the beautiful verdure all about.

The environs of Coban are beautiful, and a walk in almost any direction reveals picturesque scenery. Flowers are so abundunt that the town seems to be planted in a garden, and almost embowered in roses. This whole region is a rich field for the botanist and the ornithologist. There are many varieties of birds, many of them rare and of brilliant plumage, and they can be obtained of the Indians at a moderate sum. The finest roses of our hothouses blossom here the year round, and in the woods are the rarest orchids, which are often bought of the Indians for five cents and sold in London for hundreds of dollars.

The population of Coban is estimated at fifteen thousand, but these figures give rather an exaggerated idea of its size, as the majority are Indians, many of whom often live in a very small space. The English-speaking people were Germans, and they received us with the greatest cordiality and kindness, and did everything possible to make our stay pleasant. There were several finely educated and cultured young ladies, whose society I greatly enjoyed. Some of the Germans are owners of coffee plantations, others are merchants supplying the interior towns, and it is astonishing how many stores there are throughout the country, and what a vast amount of goods is imported, almost nothing being manufactured. Although so far removed from the civilized world, and obliged to live somewhat after the fashion of the country, still these Germans have all the comforts and luxuries of life except that they are quite deprived of society save in their own small circle; for, although they mingle somewhat with the better class of the natives, there is little affiliation between them.

No foreigners thoroughly enjoy living there. Every American and German we met in Central America was always looking forward to the time when he should return to his native land; still not one out of a hundred ever does, and those who go almost invariably return, drawn by a strange fascination which seems to hold them to this strange life.

Our arrival was quite an event in this quiet town. The Germans were glad to see any one from a civilized country, and the natives regarded us with much curiosity. We had not been in the place two hours before they knew it and were anxious to see us. They would inquire "What are they like?" and would make some excuse to come to the hotel that they might see us, the children even coming and gazing in at the windows. They seemed particularly impressed by my father's size, and whenever we appeared on the street we were gazed at with wonder and admiration, and often heard the expressions "que gordo!" ("how fat") and "pesa mucho!" ("he is very heavy"). Though they had not the slightest intention of being rude, and intended all their staring as the highest compliment, yet it was to us very unpleasant, and we found the position of "extrangeros" (foreigners) most trying and uncomfortable.

Our chief diversion was to visit the "Plaza" every morning. It was a large open square on the top of a hill in the centre of the town, enclosed by a church, cabildo and stores. In this square the Indian women sat on the ground in the hot sun, selling meat, fruit, and vegetables. It was a very curious scene, ever new and interesting, but impossible to describe, being unlike any other part of the world save the Orient. The prices were remarkable. For the smallest piece of money (a cuartilla), about three cents, we could get more oranges than we could carry; pine-apples, two for five cents; cocoanuts and bananas, three for five cents; eggs, a cent apiece; beef, twelve and a half cents a pound; and cigars, five dollars per thousand.

One afternoon we visited the cemetery, on a high hill, reached by over a hundred steps; a hard climb, but repaying us with a fine view of the surrounding country. It was a strange looking place, many of the graves being marked only by a stick, others by a rude arch of mud, and a few by monuments of whitewashed adobe. There was a small chapel, with the usual tinsel ornaments and images. Just as we reached the top of the steps the bell in the chapel began to ring violently, and, looking down, we saw mounting the hill an Indian funeral procession, headed by three or four fiddlers, and consisting of a straggling crowd, mostly women, who, according to the custom of the country, were hired to go as mourners and were making an evident effort to weep and wail.

The coffin, borne on the shoulders of four men, was a rude affair, covered with black and white paper and decorated with a skull and cross-bones, the former looking exactly like the head made by children on a "jack-lantern." The procession entered the church, where a priest stood before the altar, on which were many lighted candles, and all knelt; but we could not see that there was any service, or hear anything save the music and the bell of the chapel, which was ringing loudly.

After a few moments they proceeded to the grave and lowered the coffin, the women sobbing aloud and making an extra show of grief. This was the funeral of a wealthy Indian, for the poor mozo is merely wrapped in a "petate," and just covered with a little dirt, sometimes a toe being left sticking out of the ground.

We witnessed, too, another one of their curious customs, a religious ceremony. It was a procession of Indians carrying an image of the Virgin Mary, simply a large doll dressed beautifully in white, with many spangles, and sitting in a large chair, adorned with festoons of flowers. The image was borne by women and preceded by weird music, every one in the street kneeling before it, and remaining in that posture until it had passed.

Frequently, in passing a house in the evening, we would hear a monotonous chant, and, on looking in, for the doors were open, could see a large crowd kneeling and worshipping some image. We were told that there was very little depth to their religion; that it consisted mostly of empty show, ringing of bells, and occasional displays of fireworks. The church was large and quite handsome, but there seldom seemed to be any services held there. Sunday was the great market-day and holiday. In the afternoon there was quite a display of troops, and the band played in one of the principal squares.

We learned much of Spanish customs, and of the state of society, which is most deplorable; but as this place is simply a smaller edition of the capital, we prefer to speak of this subject later on.

Notwithstanding all that the Germans did to make our stay pleasant, as soon as we got rested we were anxious to press on; but found to our displeasure that it would take us some time to make arrangements for the new mode of travelling which we must adopt.

Up to this time I had cherished a faint hope that there would be some way to escape travelling on mule-back, of which I had the greatest dread. So far it had been possible, but between us and Guatemala there were yet nearly one hundred and fifty miles, which could be traversed only on mule-back because there was only a narrow mountain-path, merely the old trail of the Indians, very little improved from time immemorial.

Then came my greatest trial in the whole journey. Although I had sufficient courage to undertake anything else, I was very timid about riding horse-back, and this natural timidity had been increased by being thrown from a horse just before leaving home. While in Coban a party of ladies and gentlemen was made up especially for me to go and visit one of the finest estates, where there was a remarkable collection of rare orchids, but I had to beat an ignominious retreat, even after I was mounted on the horse's back, and let the rest of the party go without me. I began to think I should never get to Guatemala City. I inquired most earnestly if there was no other way; and learned that there was none save that of being carried on an Indian's back, a method sometimes employed for children and persons in feeble health. I thought even this mode of locomotion preferable to mule-back, and went so far as to try the experiment of taking a short ride in a chair strapped upon an Indian's back. But, although this fellow was a stalwart specimen, he pronounced me "too heavy"; and as the law limited an Indian's cargo to one hundred and fifteen pounds, my case was hopeless. Evidently my father and I were not designed by nature for travelling in this country. Finally, one young lady, who was also timid about riding, suggested that I might have an Indian lead my horse as she had done, telling me it would insure a great feeling of safety. This plan I decided to adopt, and tried to bring my courage up to the point of undertaking the long, hard journey.

We were now impatient to reach the capital, of which we heard high praises on every side, but found "mañana" and "no hay" great and almost insurmountable obstacles. It was more trouble to get out of that little town than it had been to prepare for our whole trip; for, although we were in a country where travelling is done almost entirely on mule-back, it was next to impossible to obtain either suitable saddles or animals; our case being particularly serious, as the mules are all small and not accustomed to carry over one hundred and fifty pounds. Finally our old friend "Dolly," called the stoutest and best mule in the country, was decided upon to carry the "heavy-weight," a pony was obtained for me, and saddles were found which some repairing made safe though not comfortable. Our baggage must be carried by Indians, but they were so plenty we supposed we could get them at a minute's notice; what was our surprise when we found we had quite a process to go through with! We had to go to the comandante and make all the arrangements through him, giving the mozos three days' notice to cook provisions (that is, tortillas) for the whole journey to and from Guatemala. We paid the comandante two dollars and fifty cents for each mozo, and for that paltry sum each was to carry a weight of seventy-five or one hundred pounds to Guatemala, and then return home, making in all a journey of nine or ten days. Furthermore, the comandante charged us not to give them generous fees, as it would establish a bad precedent. It seemed very unjust to the poor Indians to have some one else make all their bargains for them, and forbid even a little kindly charity, but the people regard them as little better than animals, and fit only for cargo-carrying, almost always addressing them as "chucho," a word used to call a dog. By dint of much urging we managed to get one mozo to go with us to lead my horse and carry our handbags, starting when we got ready, for we decided not to wait for the baggage-carriers. The comandante, on being asked if the latter would start when they agreed, said he would send an officer to arrest them the day before and put them in jail, so there could be no doubt about it.

CHAPTER VI.

ON MULE-BACK.

WE left Coban a week from the day we entered it; much to the surprise of all the people, who thought we had been wonderfully expeditious. We had hired to go with us, besides the mozo, a most excellent guide, whom we had taken great pains to secure. He was not an ordinary muleteer, but a young man from one of the coffee "finchas," and proved to be a most efficient and devoted servant. It was impossible to find a guide who could speak English, but he spoke what was far more useful in this country — the language of the Indians — and was so bright and quick to understand and anticipate our wants, that a few words were quite sufficient. He had one of the pleasantest faces I ever saw, and my father and I were both reassured the moment we saw him, for to us a good guide was of the greatest importance, as we had to depend upon him entirely, and trust wholly to his judgment. We found Melesio Guerra the embodiment of amiability, patience, and obedience, and, but for his kindness and sympathy, I believe I never could have reached Guatemala City.

For twenty or twenty-five miles the road was wide enough for a carriage, being, as far as Santa Cruz, the road we had already traversed, and we availed ourselves of the carriage for this distance. But at six o'clock in the evening we reached the spot where we must mount and begin the mode of travelling so dreaded by me. The owner of the carriage — an American — had come with us, and remained to see our mule train safely started. The guide, on a little black mule, went ahead; the Indian came next, leading my horse, and my father last, on "Dolly." The path wound up a steep hill and was very rough. We went most slowly, and by the time we began to descend were enveloped in black darkness, and the way seemed truly frightful. We could not see an inch before us; the animals, although very sure-footed, would stumble every few moments over a loose stone, or step so suddenly into a hole or deep cut as to almost throw us off their backs. I clung to the saddle until my hands were blistered, and then dismounted and walked.

At about eight o'clock we reached Santa Rosa, the little Indian village where we were to spend the night. The only incident here worth mentioning was furnished by a bright boy of seven or eight years, who occupied the third cot in the room with us, the rest of the space being entirely taken by a heap of corn. He seemed exceedingly restless, tossing about on his couch for some time, until he finally got up, and, to our surprise, proceeded to light a cigarette. With this in his mouth he retired to his cot, and, after smoking several cigarettes, finally got quiet and fell asleep. This we mention merely as illustrating the universality of smoking in this country, among men, women, and children, the boys often beginning when three or four years old; in fact, we saw one pretty little fellow of two years already addicted to the habit, in spite of whippings from his parents, who happened to be unusually strict in this matter.

The next morning we started about six o'clock, and in a few hours I lost my fear sufficiently to ride without having the horse led, much to the relief of the Indian, who evidently regarded this part of his duties as very foolish. We had not ridden far before we envied our mozo his mode of locomotion, and would gladly have changed places with him if we could. It is impossible by any words to do justice to the nature of a mule or the aches and pains of mule-back, such as we endured. A person may enjoy a gentle canter of an hour or two over a smooth road; but put that same experienced rider down in Central America, and let him ride twenty or twenty-five miles a day for five days, on a stubborn mule, up and down mountains, on a rocky road, and he will know how to appreciate a Pullman car, and never after complain of any civilized mode of travelling. But we were not even experienced riders; in fact, were not at all accustomed to it, and the motion of the mule was tiring beyond description.

At nine o'clock we reached the top of a mountain, from which we had a magnificent view; so magnificent that we paused a while to look. Before us lay a green valley all shut in by majestic mountains towering above the clouds, and bearing on their slopes little white villages which looked very fair in the distance. The largest of these our guide pointed out as Salama, the place where we should get breakfast; and, although we had learned by former experience that the saying "Distance lends enchantment" was never truer than of these Indian villages, yet this one looked so beautiful, nestling there on the mountain-side, and seemed so near, almost within a stone's throw, that we were greatly cheered by the sight, and started down the mountain with fresh courage. But the way proved long and weary, and it seemed as if we should never reach Salama, for after we descended the mountain we had to cross a long, dusty plain, and it was twelve o'clock before we reached the village — three hours from the time we saw it from the top of the mountain. It proved to be quite a large, pretty place, the best we saw in all our journey, and possessed a hotel, a long, neat looking building, with a large courtyard. The lady of the house was very pleasant and received us most politely, inviting us at once to come in and rest in a room furnished with neat cot beds and a sumptuous hammock. I immediately availed myself of this invitation. But alas for corpulency! The old story of Gulliver among the Liliputians was repeated; for the man, who was regarded as a wonder on account of his size, who even on the largest mule in the country looked as ludicrous as a boy riding a walking-stick, now, though so tired and lame he could hardly step, found, to his dismay, that the door was so small he could not pass through. The lady was very sympathetic, and urged him to try it "sideways," but it was of no use; and he had to sit on a hard bench outside the door, and have his breakfast served on the piazza, because he was too big to get into the house.

Our guide here, more thoughtful of the future than most people in this country, advised us to purchase some bread to eat with our morning cup of coffee, as this was the last place on the road where we could get it before we reached Guatemala. The bread was the same as that of Coban, already described — the one article of food in which the people excel us. It is made into all sorts of fancy shapes, and, although eaten without butter, is really delicious with a cup of coffee. We found it in all the larger towns and cities both of Central America and Mexico, and it was the one article of food we most enjoyed and were most sorry to forego.

From Salama we sent a telegram to Guatemala for a carriage to meet us Saturday morning (it was then Wednesday) at San Antonio, a few hours' ride from the city, and as far as a carriage could come, for we had no ambition to ride muleback any farther than was absolutely necessary.

At two o'clock in the afternoon, though lame, sore, and weary, we mounted again, reaching our stopping-place about 5:30. It was just at the base of a mountain, to climb which must be our next task, and we had been told by everybody it was the highest mountain in all the way. Besides the thought of this to trouble us, there were many fleas to torment us; and ever after this until we once more got into the United States, we suffered from these troublesome insects. The woman of the house where we stopped had the goître, and we saw several men and women, in this part of the country, afflicted with this disease. It is a swelling of the front and sides of the neck, sometimes reaching a great size so as even to hang down upon the chest. When large, its weight presses upon the windpipe and causes difficulty of breathing, alteration of the voice, and a bad cough, finally ending in consumption, apoplexy, or suffocation. We inquired the cause of this strange disease, and always received the answer, "the water," which hardly seemed possible to us, for the water drank here is that of mountain streams, which seem clear and sparkling and pure. The disease is found only in mountainous countries, being common in Switzerland, in dark, deep valleys, where the air is cold and moist and the water contains lime or other alkaline substances.

Next morning we climbed the high mountain, which was at least three miles up and six down; the ascent took over an hour and the descent more than two. The coming down was very tiresome, for we had to keep ourselves braced every moment, not daring to change in the least our position lest we be thrown over the mules' heads; and the road was narrow and steep, with some deep cuts which were really frightful. But we reached the bottom safely about ten o'clock, and found a mud hut, where the housekeeper and head of the family was a pretty girl of about fifteen years. As usual, we flung ourselves into hammocks to wait for breakfast, but the delay was longer than usual, for the girl had no one to help her; and to get breakfast in this country is a long task. Everything is cooked over a little charcoal fire; and if they have a dozen eggs to fry or twenty tortillas to bake, only one is cooked at a time.

All the afternoon we were travelling on the plains; it was very hot, and the road was dusty and uninteresting, part of the way a narrow path over a ravine, whose depth, however, was slight compared with what we saw afterwards.

All the way we found the same kind of villages and the same lack of accommodations as in our journey from Panzos to Coban, though our excellent guide relieved us from all care and trouble, and made us as comfortable as possible, furnishing us with one luxury which we fully appreciated, a calabash of water every morning, in which to bathe our faces; so we did not have to hunt around as before for a running stream, and go with dirty faces if we could not find one. The road was even more mountainous than before, especially after the first day. In fact, this range is remarkable for its lack of valleys; and, with the exception of one day, when we rode for a while on a hot, dusty plain, we were climbing mountains all the time, having no sooner descended one than we had to ascend another. In our ascent we were often among the clouds hovering about the mountain, and for a while would be enveloped in fog and mist, or even rain, until we mounted above them into clear sunlight again. Being in higher regions, we saw less of luxuriant tropical verdure but more sugar and banana plantations, "haciendas" (cattle ranches), and fields of corn and cactus. There were very few signs of agriculture or labor of any kind, fields often rich and fertile being entirely uncultivated. No matter what time of the day we stopped at a house to rest, the men were almost invariably at home doing nothing, save now and then we found one weaving in a simple hand-loom the coarse cloth of which the Indian's dress is made. The women seemed more industrious than the men, for they were housekeepers; and the noise of the Indian housewife patting her tortillas in preparation for breakfast was the only sound that ever broke the silence of our quiet morning rides. For what need have men to work in a land of perpetual summer, where fruits grow wild, and a small piece of ground will produce frijoles and corn, their sole living; where branches and stout vines from the woods furnish the framework of their houses, mud the covering, and palm leaves the thatching for the roof? They come up idle and careless in the sunshine, marry, grow old, and die, never having advanced a step beyond their fathers, nor, to all appearance, had a longing for better things. Yet there was never a more docile, kind-hearted, happy people in the world, and who shall say they are not much better off than we, with our artificial wants, and strivings after the impossible?

The third night we spent at Las Canoas, a pretty, picturesque spot by a river, but the comandante was the first and only one in all the journey not to show us the greatest politeness. He seemed entirely absorbed in his own imagined greatness, and took no notice of us. If we had reported him to President Barrios, he would have lost his place and perhaps his head, for the President especially instructed all his officials throughout the country to show the utmost courtesy and kindness to strangers. We were already quite familiar with Barrios' face, for his picture hung in every cabildo, and we often heard praises of his government.

All about the cabildo here was a great crowd of Indians, as many as forty or fifty, and they made a very picturesque sight partaking of their evening meal. The women built the little fire of sticks and warmed up the tortillas, while each one placed a small calabash of water in the fire to be heated, for, as we learned, they always drink their water hot. This seemed strange and we asked our guide the reason. He said, "It is good for the stomach," which made us wonder if the recent hot water remedy had its origin among the Indians.

The fourth day, at half-past six, we mounted again, passing just out of the village a fine bridge, which surprised us very much, as it was the only one of any size in the whole journey, though we saw many places where bridges were greatly needed, both over streams and gulleys.

We were now constantly meeting more travellers than before, and their number increased as we neared the capital. There were companies of soldiers, both men and women on mule-back, and large bands of mozos, including boys, carrying burdens almost as large as themselves, and it was an ever new and interesting study to look into their faces, and observe their queer gait, by which they make almost as good time as a mule. In fact, the mozo who went with us made every day the same stations we did, not being behind us more than an hour. It is surprising how perfectly erect these Indians are, though they have to go half bent under their cargo; the moment their burden is dropped they stand as straight as an arrow, and we never once saw an Indian bowed over. We got accustomed to their dark color, and grew even to like it after a while. Very often we came upon a large group of them under a wide-spreading tree by a running brook, resting and preparing a meal, and there was never a more interesting, picturesque wayside scene than they presented.

The fourth day it was very hot and dusty; we were lame and weary, and my father suffered much from thirst. His continual cry all day was "agua, agua," and he halted for water at every hut, running stream, and Indian band. We found only very small villages in the way, and no signs of labor or cultivation. The first hut we came to was in the midst of a large banana plantation, with no other house in sight. Seeing the guide about to dismount I asked, "How far is it to San Bernato?" (the place where we were to breakfast). He answered, "This is San Bernato"; and, sure enough, the one house was dignified with the rank and title of a village. The population, however, was not altogether insignificant, for there was a very large family of dirty children, and it was the only really untidy house in which we ever ate.

About noon, being warm and tired, we stopped again, at one of a group of three or four houses, also constituting a village, with a long name, "Talpichi Grande." We were received most cordially by the people, who showed us the greatest attention. There was little they could do, for they had little to do with; but they could not have treated us better if we had been kings.

In this house they manufactured "chicha," the favorite drink of the Indians, tasting like sweet cider, but said to be quite intoxicating. In fact, we had an illustration of its effect at this very house, where an Indian was talking very volubly in Spanish, a language he would have probably disdained in his sober moments; for such is the hatred for the Spaniards among the Indians, that, although they as a rule understand the language, they will not speak it, save in the large cities, and where it is absolutely necessary.

As usual, on entering these houses our first

thought was to rest; and I had a new experience here, even for this country. The single cot was already partly occupied by a sitting hen, but she seemed not at all disturbed by my approach, and I was so tired and had grown so accustomed to the prevailing style of living that nothing surprised me, and I actually shared the pillow some time with my feathered friend before the ludicrousness of the situation occurred to me, and I began to wonder what our Boston friends would say if they knew the style in which we were travelling.

After we got rested enough to move, we mounted again, though the people urged us not to go on in the heat, and offered us every inducement to remain; but we never could stay long in their wretched huts, and preferred moving on to resting there. Just before we went our mozo arrived; and seeing the "chicha," he asked most eagerly for a "cuartilla." We left him drinking out of a large bowl, and when we saw him again, at night, its effects were evident in his attempts to converse in Spanish, though he had never before ventured to address us.

We very soon left the plains, and resumed our journey on a narrow mountain path, the precipice ever growing deeper and deeper as we wound around the mountain, and gradually ascended. At three o'clock we reached the very top, where there was a little village of three or four houses, and where we had planned to pass the night, but it was such a barren, lonely place, without a cabildo, or even "zacate" for the mules, that we felt as if we could not stay, and must try to reach another station before night. How anxiously I questioned the guide, but he said there was not even a hut between there and San Antonio, which was so far it could not be reached until very late, and that the road was too dangerous for travelling in the dark. So we reluctantly dismounted, and passed as best we could the long, weary afternoon, sitting on a hard bench, listening to the soughing of the wind in the pine trees, watching a drove of lean, hungry pigs trying to steal corn from our mules; or, as usual when we made a long stop, giving the guide a lesson in English, for he was very anxious to learn, and I was glad to help him, on account of his devotion and faithfulness. The pronunciation troubled him but little, and he learned very quickly. The Spanish seem to have a wonderful ability for acquiring our language, and, as a nation, speak it remarkably well. A Frenchman or German, no matter how well he knows English, will almost invariably betray his nationality by his accent; but a Spaniard speaks it as if it were his native tongue. Our first Spanish friend, Emilio Carranza, knew very little English, but the few sentences he used were spoken as perfectly as if he had been an American.

We got our dinner at one of the houses, and were happy in the addition of a bowl of honey, which we bought for a "medio" (six and one fourth cents), but we were greatly troubled to get a drink of water, as the soil was clayey, and the water turbid and disagreeable. About three miles before we reached this place, we stopped by the road and drank at a spring of clearest water, and, as there were plenty of Indians about, whose highest wages were a real a day, with the guide's help we engaged one, giving him two reals to go to this spring for some water. He was away about an hour, just about the time necessary, received his pay, and departed before we tasted the water, which we were delighted to obtain. What was our surprise to find the same muddy, disagreeable, unhealthy water which was right at hand! That Indian had deceived us well. He started off in the right direction, but had come back and stayed by the spring behind the house, and, when he thought sufficient time had elapsed, had dipped up the water, brought it to us, and received pay for two days' work.

The place where we were to spend the night was an open shed made of a few boughs bound together with vines, with no door, with no covering of mud or thatching for the roof, and with wide-open spaces where we looked out upon the sky. In fact, it was just the same as sleeping out of doors, and was so cold from the high elevation that all our wraps were not sufficient to keep us warm. We repaired to our hammocks at dark, the guide and mozo lying on the ground near by; but for us there was no sleep. The mules never for a moment ceased champing corn all night; the whole drove of pigs were squealing, and grunting, and running about the shed; and all the dogs in the village, in numbers more than the inhabitants, were barking incessantly. What wonder that in that dreary spot, during the hours of that sleepless night, one of us, more timid than the other, heard strange noises, and half believed a band of Indians were coming to overpower us, as they might easily have done, and reaped a rich harvest, for we were all unarmed and unprotected, and our bags contained much money. One thing we know: had we been in Mexico under such circumstances, we should never have seen daylight again. Is it any wonder, then, that we have an affection for the people of Guatemala?

Finally we concluded it was no use to try longer to sleep, and, though it was not quite three o'clock, decided to get up. We called the guide, who, at the word "señor," was on his feet to do our bidding, as amiable and ready as if it were broad daylight, and we had not disturbed him out of a sound sleep. He immediately began to rouse the mozo, which was not so easy a task; for to him the ground was a soft couch, and he was sleeping soundly. He grunted and groaned, and was fully fifteen minutes getting on his feet and kindling the pitch-pine knots for a light in the darkness. Melesio also aroused the woman of the house for our coffee, and saddled the mules. We took our coffee and tortillas in the room where the man and boy of the family were still sleeping. We gave the woman for her trouble a generous fee, with which she was highly pleased, and proceeded to put it in the bed under her sleeping husband's head. We laughingly told her not to put it there as he might get it, and it was money she had earned herself. She appreciated the joke, though it was told mostly by gestures, but seemed to have true ideas of the matrimonial relation, and was nothing loath to trust her all with him.

This had taken but little time and we were soon ready to mount; but knowing we were on the top of a mountain, we dared not venture in the blackness of night, and even our fearless guide, so accustomed to the road, did not wish to start, and said the way was steeper and narrower than we had yet seen. How anxiously we looked for dawn, but no light came; the sky was bright with stars, and the glorious constellation of the Southern Cross, our only reward for a sleepless night, was still above the horizon. Each time our fire of pitch-pine knots went out it seemed darker than before, and we could only wait impatiently for day. At last, though but little past four, we ventured, hoping the dawn would soon come to us on the way. We went very slowly, in the dim light hardly able to see each other. The sunrise was entirely shut out by the great mountains surrounding us, but gradually the light of day came and revealed to us the awfulness of our situation. We were on a narrow shelf of rock overhanging a terrible precipice. Words utterly fail to portray the grandeur and awfulness of this great mountain gorge through which we were riding. The path, on the very side of a high mountain, was so narrow that two mules could barely pass, and the overhanging branches of the trees often brushed against us with such force as almost to throw us from our mules. On one side was a perfectly straight wall of rock, on the other a sheer declivity of hundreds of feet as straight as a plummet line. At the foot of the precipice a mountain stream roared over the rocks, its deafening noise adding to the terrors of the place, and from it arose another chain of mountains, seeming to hem us in completely, with no hope of escape. There were many bad places in the path, some so frightful that we dismounted and walked; great gulleys washed out by the water, and deep cuts covered with loose stones, where it seemed as if the mule's feet would surely slip and precipitate us to a sudden death. What was more trying still, the mules would go on the *very edge* overhanging the precipice, and no amount of reining could prevent it. In fact if we reined them in toward the wall they would stop altogether; and as it was no place to have a tussle, we held our breath and let them have their own way. One false step or the least crumbling of the earth and we should have been hurled to the awful depth below, as we knew had happened to more than one luckless traveller in this place. Melesio went ahead very calmly, so well known and familiar a place having no terrors for him. In one spot where we bent sharply around the mountain, and the path was scarcely wide enough for the mule's feet, he turned around and told us to look down. Our heads fairly whirled at a mere glance. The frightful depth was enough to make the strongest nerves quail and the stoutest heart faint. Had we been suddenly transplanted to this spot, we should certainly have been paralyzed with terror; but as it was we rode as if under a spell, not realizing until afterwards either the dangers or the magnificence of the scene. Every time we bent around the mountain we hoped to see the road descend, but still we went on and on hour after hour, and we were so weary after a sleepless night, so worn and exhausted with over a hundred miles in the saddle, that it seemed as if we should never get down from the dangerous and toilsome height. Finally, about ten o'clock, the path gradually descended, then broadened out, a brisk trot of a few minutes brought us to San Antonio, and our mule-back was done. How thankful we were to see a carriage awaiting us, and how gladly we dismounted for the last time from those mules, none but Melesio Guerra can ever fully appreciate. He understood it all, and expressed it in brief but forcible Spanish, "No mas mulas."

In the family with whom we breakfasted were several very beautiful young girls; dark of course, but with perfect features, long, abundant hair, and lustrous black eyes. They ministered to all our wants with the grace and politeness so characteristic of the Spanish.

By the time we were ready to start the mozo had arrived. My father gave him his broad straw hat and as generous a fee as he dared, advising him not to spend it for "chicha." This kindness was too much even for an Indian's stolidity, and his whole face beamed with gratitude as he said, "Dios se lo paga" ("God will pay you"). Money seemed poor return for Melesio's kindness, but was our only means of recompense. He had proved a most valuable and efficient guide and friend, and will have our lasting gratitude. He had become quite attached to us and looked sad at parting, giving us a hearty handshake as he said "good-bye" to my father and "adios niña" to me. To him and Emilio Carranza, these two simple but noble youths of Guatemala, I feel that I owe the greatest debt of gratitude of my whole life. May God in his mercy watch over and protect them wherever they may be!

CHAPTER VII.

THE CAPITAL.

It was only a short ride from San Antonio to Guatemala City. The carriage which met us, like everything in this country, was peculiar; a covered vehicle, with seats arranged as in an omnibus, drawn by four little mules not much bigger than rats, and about as ungovernable. The driver was a bright, black-eyed boy, and showed much skill in managing these untamed creatures. No carriage was ever so welcome as that one, and it was well for us that its owner did not know how we valued it, for my father was so tired of muleback that he declared he would have had this carriage for that short time if it had taken the last cent he possessed.

We arrived in Guatemala City as tired, dusty, and wretched specimens of humanity as ever entered its gates. Our first impressions were those of astonishment at seeing a city so large, and so superior to anything we had yet seen in the country, or even imagined from description.

It is called, on account of its prosperity, the Paris of Central America, or, as they say there, "Pequeña Paris." It is situated in a broad, fertile valley, almost entirely surrounded by deep "barrancas," or ravines, and has an elevation of five thousand two hundred and seventy feet above the sea.

The climate is simply perfect, the finest in the world. It is neither too warm nor too cold; seldom above eighty or below sixty degrees, with scarcely ten degrees difference between winter and summer, or, more properly speaking, between the rainy and dry seasons. It is, in fact, an ideal climate, just adapted for gardens of roses and violets the year round. We were there in the dry season, and it was a luxury we appreciated never to have to wonder, when planning an expedition, if the weather would favor us. We were sure of bright sunshine every day. The rainy season lasts from May to October, and we were assured by those living there that it is not at all disagreeable. They have no long dreary rain-storms such as we have here, but at about the same time every afternoon a tremendous shower of rain, after which the sky is clear again. Much is said by every traveller to Mexico about the fineness of the climate; but visiting both places in the same winter, we had an excellent chance to compare the two, and, though they are similar, we pronounce most decidedly in favor of Guatemala as being both more healthful and agreeable.

The present capital was built in 1775, after the destruction (by an earthquake) of the former capital, now called Antigua, and has a population of about forty-five thousand. The streets are wide, regular, and well paved. There are lines of horse-cars running to all parts, and just the night before we left the electric light was introduced for lighting the city. There are many public buildings, parks, squares, and beautiful gardens. It seemed to us, on the whole, a very pleasant city, and we enjoyed a two weeks' stay there very much.

The houses, though mostly of one story, on account of the earthquakes, are many of them large and comfortable. The architecture of the houses is that of southern Spain. They are all built in the form of a hollow square, and the interior court, containing trees and flowers, is often very beautiful. They are not at all prepossessing from the exterior, presenting to the street a blank white wall with barred windows and a huge solid door like that of a prison; but the moment the door is opened in response to the noise of the great knocker, the visitor is ushered into the interior court and into a scene of verdure and beauty.

We stopped at the "Gran Hotel," which proved to be the best we found in the whole journey. The proprietors were Germans, and most excellent gentlemen. They spoke English. and we were rejoiced to hear it once more, not having heard a word for five days, except what we spoke ourselves. The Germans seem to be wonderful linguists; nearly every one we met could speak, besides his own language, English, French, Spanish, and Italian, all of which are quite essential to one doing business here, it is such a cosmopolitan city. In the dining-room we often heard all these different languages from the tables about us. The landlady was a very pleasant young German woman; and as I was the only lady in the hotel, she took compassion on my situation, and did her best to make it pleasant. We had a most amusing time trying to converse, for we had no language in common. She knew very little English, I knew little German, and neither of us knew Spanish well. But she was very lively, and we made up in laughing what we lacked in conversation, and enjoyed each other very much.

The building itself, one of the few two-story houses of the city, is very beautiful. It was formerly a private residence of a very wealthy family, but its owner, we were told, was banished by Barrios as a real or supposed accomplice in some conspiracy, and now the daughters who once lived in this really palatial home are poor seamstresses. There were balconies all round the interior, overlooking the garden, which contained peach, orange, palm trees, beautiful flowers, and a fountain, also some little green paroquets, and a lovely little blue-jay, so tame that he would allow his head to be stroked, and would even perch on your shoulder.

The fare was good, and to us seemed excellent, for we were actually hungry. The order of meals is entirely different from ours, as well as the manner of serving. From 7 to 8, coffee and "pan dulce," in your room if you wish; breakfast, 9:30 to 11; dinner, 3:30 to 6. For breakfast there were always cold meats, salad, eggs (to order), frijoles, fried plantains, pancakes, with honey, and coffee or chocolate. For dinner, soup, "olla" (sort of boiled dinner), fish or game, poultry, roast beef, "dulce" (sweets), fruit, and coffee or chocolate. The chocolate is that of the country, and very nice, though always flavored with cinnamon.

It is the custom to serve only one thing at a time, and this is rather harassing to an American, especially the fact that it is impossible to get a cup of coffee until everything else has been removed. Over their cup of coffee the gentlemen sit and smoke at their leisure, alternating a sip of the favorite beverage with a puff of their cigar.

A colored boy, travelling as servant to an American gentleman, furnished us some amusement in his struggles with Spanish, or rather without it, for he couldn't speak a word; and as the servants of the hotel spoke nothing else, he had rather a lonesome time. One day he got together the two fellows who took care of the rooms (for the "chambermaids" are all men in this country), and proceeded to give them a lesson in English. The part we heard was quite laughable.

He was making them repeat, over and over, "Me speak English," and "y-e-s — yes," though what good it would do them to spell this one word, when they could neither read nor spell their own language, was a mystery.

For the first three days we did nothing but eat and sleep, being completely exhausted. The day after our arrival (Sunday) Carnival began, and there was little inducement for us to go out, as the whole city was given up to the perfect license which reigns during the three days. As far as we could observe, Carnival seemed here to amount to very little, except a perfect "bonanza" for rude boys, who paraded the streets, often in companies of twenty or thirty, throwing at everybody indiscriminately, flour, eggs, paint, and showers from squirt-guns, with which they were all armed. Many of the ladies shut themselves in their houses during the whole time, for this crowd is no respecter of persons. One night, as we were watching the fun from the roof of the hotel, we saw the Spanish minister and wife, just entering the theatre, rudely assaulted by a company of these boys. The more one appears vexed at this treatment, the worse it is for him. The best way is to submit calmly and quietly, if possible. The police give orders that strangers shall not be molested, but still one can never feel perfectly sure, though we went out several times without being at all troubled.

After Carnival we began to receive many callers, both Germans and Americans, particularly the latter, who were most glad to welcome some of their own countrymen. It seemed to us almost like getting home to meet some of our own people once more, especially a few from good New England, and I found most pleasant companions in several young ladies who very kindly went about with me sight-seeing, showing me all the places of interest, their knowledge of the city being a great advantage to me. The American minister, Mr. Hall, and his family received us most cordially, entertained us many times at their house, and did all in their power to make our stay pleasant. Mr. Hall is a very able man, and, what is very unusual and speaks highly in his praise, is much esteemed and beloved by all, both natives and foreigners. He has lived much in Spanish countries, and speaks Spanish as well as English, which is a very great advantage. Mrs. Hall is a Cuban by birth, a very cultured and highly esteemed lady.

There are in the city many squares and gardens, one in particular containing a fine collection of cactuses, some much taller than a man. The principal square is called the "Plaza Mayor," and includes, besides the governmental buildings, the great cathedral, a fine imposing building, similar to the cathedral of Mexico, and, like it, built by the Spaniards.

The market, which so interested us in every town, was here a large building, the centre being occupied by the Indian women, selling all sorts of provisions, and the exterior surrounded by little booths in which were sold all kinds of fabrics made by the Indians, as well as many cheap imported articles which the Indians buy. It was always a busy and interesting scene, though we saw some curious and anything but agreeable sights; for instance, in the pauses of trade, women nursing their babes or searching industriously the heads of their children with a large, coarse, wooden comb. None of these traders ever have any paper with which to do up a bundle, but instead there are all through the market young girls with baskets on their heads, whose business it is to carry your purchases for you. There is no difficulty in having this sort of express; for there is a host of girls, and as soon as you enter the market they besiege you for a job. They will follow you about for half a day if you like, direct you where to go, advise you what to buy, and then, when you have finished, carry the whole to the hotel for five cents. One thing we learned about shopping, with everybody else who comes here, never to give more than half what is first charged. Bartering, however disagreeable it may seem, is absolutely essential here. Indeed if you do not do it, the Indians themselves laugh at you and call you "green Americans."

There are many fine churches, built by the Spaniards; in fact, with the exception of Mexico, they are the finest in Spanish America. The exterior is beautifully ornamented, and the interior contains magnificent altars, beautiful paintings and frescoes, and many images of Christ, Mary and innumerable saints. Some of these images are very beautiful, but the greater portion represent the agonies of Christ, and are painful to contemplate.

These churches were established in the sixteenth century, by the Jesuits, who became very corrupt and powerful, getting everything, property and government, under their control. In 1870, with the rise of the "Liberal Party," their power began to be broken, and when Barrios became President, in 1872, he declared the order extinct, broke up the monasteries, banishing and killing many priests and nuns, and confiscating all their property. This he recognized as absolutely essential if Guatemala was to be anything of a power or have any place among other nations. Under the then existing state of affairs no commerce or enterprise was possible, no business men would engage in any pursuits there, and a country with rich resources and wonderful possibilities was lying stagnant, corrupt and powerless.

But although the power of the order is broken the religion still exists and has its hold on the people. Even those who have renounced the faith, and glory in the name of "Infidel," are at heart Catholics still.

There is one small Protestant mission in the city, the only one in the country. It has been started but a few years, but has been the most successful mission ever planted in Spanish America. The minister is a very able man from central New York. There is also connected with the church a mission school, which has attracted the people on account of their anxiety to learn English. Both the church and the school received the hearty support of Barrios; not so much because he favored this form of religion as because he recognized in it a civilizing and progressive power, the power he admired above all others. To show his approval, he even went so far as to send his own children for a time to the school, and in every way helped and encouraged it. Since he favored it no one dared offer any opposition, for his word was law; but the people called it in derision a "Protestanteria" (a shop for making Protestants).

Guatemala has, comparatively speaking, good schools throughout the country, but especially at the capital, where many come to be educated. President Barrios made a law that every Indian should learn to read and write, though there were not many to support him in this good work. One German lady expressed her opposition in the strongest terms. She said, "It is almost impossible to get any servants now, for they are all in the schools! What does an Indian want to learn to read and write for? It'll never do him any good."

There are two large "colegios" in this city, a visit to which proved very interesting. They were formerly extensive convents, but Barrios converted them into schools. All the appointments are complete; there are maps, charts, diagrams, and apparatus requisite for a good thorough advanced education. Of course they are not equal to ours, but are fine for the country. Both schools are provided with large courts for out of door recreation, an ample hall and gymnasium. Attached to the boys' school, which is the largest and numbers about three hundred pupils, is a fine large museum, containing a valuable collection; a zoölogical garden, containing all the birds and animals of the country; and another garden, full of rare and beautiful trees, plants, and flowers.

The city has quite a large, handsome theatre, and we went one evening in company with the American minister's family. A French opera company was there for the season, and they received a subsidy of $20,000 from the government. The play was not specially enjoyable, but the whole scene was interesting, the arrangement of the theatre being very different from ours. The main body of the house was occupied entirely by men, and, it is needless to say, was completely emptied between acts. The rest of the house is made up of boxes, spaces partitioned off, seating either five or six persons. The American minister's box, in which we sat, was in the first balcony; that of President Barrios on the first floor, facing the stage. There were many fine toilettes — for the ladies go in full dress, and the foreigners and natives of the wealthiest class dress very elegantly, having their costumes direct from Paris. Mrs. Barrios was present with one of her governesses, and looked very beautiful, attired in a rich silk and resplendent with diamonds.

CHAPTER VIII.

A BULL FIGHT.

VERY soon after our arrival in Guatemala we heard much of the great national Spanish amusement, the bull fight, which occurred every afternoon at four o'clock during Carnival, although it usually took place only on Sundays. These were to be the last of the season, as Lent began immediately after Carnival. Our friend the proprietor of the river steamers was still in Guatemala, and offered to serve as escort if we wished to go, but added that we should probably be disappointed, as there was usually very little excitement attending a bull fight, that the bulls were quite tame, and the killing of them a most brutal exhibition, which none but a Spaniard could enjoy; still, as we had never been, and it was the great national sport, we ought to go. This and this alone was our reason for going. With a desire to learn as much as possible of the character and customs of the people, we felt that this their characteristic institution could not be overlooked. This zeal for knowledge, however, was very severely punished, for the witnessing of this barbarous spectacle was a most painful experience.

Since it was Carnival we were cautioned not to wear anything that water, ink, or flour would spoil. This caution, in our case, was entirely unnecessary, as the mozos with our luggage had not yet arrived, and the suits worn in the long ride had become so dilapidated and discolored as to present no temptations to the players at Carnival, who left us quite unmolested.

As we came in sight of the "Plaza de Toros" we saw a large crowd of people and a great many policemen near one of the windows where tickets were sold, and heard the English language spoken in the loudest and most vehement manner. As we came nearer we saw the cause of all this tumult to be two young Americans, from Massachusetts, evidently thoroughly enraged. They were covered completely from head to foot with flour, water, and gorgeous paint, and, with coats off and fists doubled up, were gesticulating wildly as they poured forth a torrent of angry words. But they might just as well have been talking to "stocks and stones," for not one in that crowd understood a single word they said. As we came up one of them was just saying, in the most forcible manner of which the English language is capable, that "if he could not walk the streets without being assaulted in that manner, he would know the reason then and there, if he had to lick the whole Republic." We got their attention at once by a word of English, and explained that this was merely the custom in Carnival, and that it was better to take it all quietly and good-naturedly than to undertake the annihilation of Guatemala. Thereupon they calmed down, bought their tickets, and went inside.

This is an illustration of the great courtesy and patience shown to strangers by the officials — far greater than that practised in our own country — for if it had been natives making such a disturbance they would have been locked up immediately.

The arena is after the same model as the old Greek and Roman amphitheatres, for the Spaniard inherited this custom from his Roman ancestors, the bull fight being the only representative at present of the old gladiatorial combats.

The building is circular, about fifteen feet high,

of the same material as the houses, but gorgeously painted with red, and decorated with flags. A band of music plays outside while the gay throng is assembling, and crowds of soldiers and policemen are seen with something of a feeling of relief, for a spell of horror comes upon one even on approaching the place.

Inside is the large circular ring, the place of the combat, open to the sky but enclosed by a moderately high fence, in front of which are placed at intervals wooden guards, and behind these the fighters may retreat when hotly pursued by the bull. The seats are raised as in a circus or theatre, and the uppermost circle of seats is roofed over so as to be sheltered from the sun, and for these an extra price is charged.

The ring was capable of seating three or four thousand people, and the throng gathered there included the wealth and aristocracy of the city as well as the poorer classes; but, what seemed most surprising, parents came bringing their little innocent children to witness this brutal spectacle. The wealthy ladies were dressed elegantly; the whole audience had a holiday air, and seemed to be in just the liveliest and happiest mood. There was never a more brilliant throng than assembles at a Spanish bull fight.

When the time arrived for the performance to begin, the band took its place inside, and the crowd, in which the boy element was conspicuous, showed its impatience by stamping feet, clapping hands, and the usual demonstrations shown in our theatres. Finally the gate opened and the company entered amid music from the band. The company consisted of six performers on foot, gorgeously dressed in tight-fitting suits of red, green, blue, or crimson, richly trimmed with lace and gilt, with little black velvet caps, white stockings, and long capes of two colors draped gracefully over the shoulder. Next came two men, called "picadores," on horse-back, also richly dressed, and bearing long pikes. Behind them came three mules, all of the same size, harnessed together, furnished with jingling bells, gayly caparisoned with saddles of red and white, and driven by several boys cracking enormously long whip-lashes. They coursed the ring, presenting a brilliant appearance; the performers made a low bow to the master of ceremonies, and then all withdrew except the six actors, one of whom repaired to a side door to await the coming of the bull, doubtless with far less trepidation than we felt, who were witnessing our first bull fight.

The animal came with a plunge, and this man threw into his back a barbed wire, surmounted by a gay bouquet of tissue paper. The bull dashed for the men in the ring, who slipped dexterously out of the way, and, as soon as he became a little calmer, waved their gay-colored capes in front of him. Then the riders came in to excite him further by goading him with their long spears. This use of horses is one of the very worst features, for the poor things are blindfolded and are forced by their riders up to the very horns of the bull, where they are completely at his mercy, and are often killed.

The next performance was the thrusting of the "banderillas,"—long darts gayly adorned with tissue paper, which were thrown, two at a time, into his shoulders. All this was to infuriate the bull, but this poor creature seemed very tame, and, after chasing some of the men until they disappeared behind their wooden guards, looked about in a dazed, helpless way, that was truly pitiful, evidently suffering pain, with blood streaming down his sides from the darts. The audience, however, felt no sympathy for him, only great derision because he was no fiercer, and kept crying, "otro toro, otro toro" ("another bull, another bull"), and calling for "la musica" to enliven their flagging spirits. Still the actors tried to enrage him by waving before him their colored capes, and the horsemen would frequently goad him with the long pike, until our only wish was that they would kill him and put him out of his misery.

The killing of the bull is really a skilful and wonderful feat, when well done. The weapon used is a sword about two and a half feet long, and the actor has to conform to certain conditions. He cannot take the bull unawares, the bull must be in a position on the offensive, coming to attack him, and the sword must be plunged in a particular spot back of the head and in front of the fore shoulder, so as to pass through the heart. After the bull becomes somewhat weary, the "matador" prepares to kill him. The red cape waved in front of him attracts his attention and he makes a rush for the man, who, without stirring from his position, as the bull's head is lowered to toss him in the air, dexterously moves his body sideways to clear the bull's horns, plunges the sword as quick as a flash, and gets out of the way.

The "matador" in this instance was most skilful, and quick as lightning plunged the sword to its hilt through the heart. The bull stopped in twice his length, and fell dead. Then the gayly harnessed mules were driven in on a run, and the lifeless body was dragged quickly around the circuit of the ring, and finally through the door, in the midst of cracking whips, jingling bells, gay music, and tremendous applause.

This performance is usually repeated until four bulls are killed, with no variation except what the disposition of the bull provides. At this fight the second bull was lively enough to upset a horse and rider occasionally; but the third one was of an entirely different character, such as is rarely witnessed. He came into the ring with rage and fury, as if bent upon avenging the unjust death of the other two, plunging through the gate as soon as it was open; so quickly that the performer failed to thrust the wired bouquet. But there was no need of goading or torturing to excite his wrath, and the actors themselves seemed to have a wholesome fear of him. It was some time before they got an opportunity to throw the "banderillas," and when the first two tore into his flesh he stopped short, shook his body to try to get rid of them, pawing the ground and frothing at the mouth in his rage. As one of the horsemen ventured to ride toward him, the bull made a rush, struck the horse in the side, disembowelling him, and throwing the rider to the ground. Then, without slackening his speed, he rushed at the other horse, turned him head over heels, and threw the rider ten feet into the air. The man fell flat on his back with great violence, and lay there stunned, at the mercy of the bull. He was then the only man in the ring, all the others having retreated behind their guards; but one of them quickly appeared, to attract the bull's attention. As the bull rushed for him he dexterously stepped aside, and ran as fast as he could; but just as he was going to jump behind the guard, he was caught on the horns of the bull, and thrown violently. He was carried out of the ring, still alive, but died from his injuries next day. The bull then returned to his first victim, still lying stunned on the ground, drove his horns into the man's head and killed him, thus proving himself master of the situation by the death of two men and one horse.

This fearful tragedy, as far as we could observe, had no particular effect upon the audience, which seemed entirely unmoved by any feelings of horror or pity. The killing of the bull was not attempted. Instead, he was lassooed, bound with ropes, and removed from the ring. It was then our dinner hour; and having seen already too much, we withdrew, assured by our friend that we had witnessed a genuine bull fight.

After the performance it is customary to raffle for the bodies of the slain bulls, the numbers of the reserved seats being placed in a hat, and four drawn out. Then the ring is given up to the audience, several bulls are let in, and the boys and any who wish go in and amuse themselves.

As to the moral effects on a nation of such a barbarous institution as the bull fight, it is quite unnecessary to speak. The fact that an audience of men, women, and children, can not only contemplate with calmness, but actually enjoy seeing an animal goaded and tortured, and finally killed, to see noble horses wantonly sacrificed, and even human life recklessly thrown away, shows a horrible and almost incredible condition of society. How a Spaniard can enjoy it — and none but a Spaniard can — is beyond the comprehension of any other human being! Equally difficult is it to appreciate the manner in which this amusement is aggrandized by the Spaniards. It is considered a profession worthy of all the respect and admiration given to any branch of the arts. There are certain prescribed laws which all the actors must obey, and every matador is criticised as carefully as a star actor or opera singer in America. But the Spaniard alone regards this sport as an art. For an American, with any feeling whatever, there is no more shocking or harrowing spectacle than a bull fight. The feelings of indignation, horror, and disgust, excited in one first witnessing a bull fight are beyond description, or even the power of imagination. No wonder that in lands where bull fights occur revolutions are frequent, and human life is esteemed of but little value. It is to be hoped that they will soon become a thing of the past, and it seems strange that they have not long ago become so. There is a slight move in this direction. In Spain, the laws prohibit the establishment of any new arenas, and in Mexico they are prohibited altogether in what is called the "Federal District," in which the City of Mexico is situated; but within a few miles of the city they are held, and the immense number of vehicles of all kinds, besides large numbers of horse-cars, and numerous horsemen who eagerly repair to the spot, shows most eloquently the hold this barbarous amusement has on most of the people. Foreigners generally witness one bull fight, but rarely care to see the performance repeated.

CHAPTER IX.

ANTIGUA AND A BURIED CITY.

THIRTY miles from Guatemala are the sites of the two former capitals, one buried by an eruption from the volcano "Agua" in 1541, the other destroyed by earthquake in 1775. A regular coach, or "diligencia," as it is called, runs there from Guatemala; but the pleasanter way is to hire a team and start early in the morning, for the ride is a long, hot, and dusty one.

We started at half-past five in the morning, in company with a gentleman and his wife whose acquaintance we made in Guatemala. The best team we could obtain was the same one in which we had come from San Antonio. We had the same youthful driver, but two stout mules, instead of the little, black, rat-like creatures we had before.

The ride in the fresh morning air was delightful. We passed one of the most beautiful gardens of the city; the "Castello," a great Spanish

.astle on a high hill; and thence by a broad, smooth driveway through the gates of the city.

At this time of the day the road was thronged with Indians loaded with all sorts of merchandise, wood, vegetables, fruit, pottery, hay, coal, everything needed in the capital, to which they were going from the little villages all around to sell their supplies in the market. They always go in groups; the men by themselves and the women by themselves, a man and a woman never walking together unless married. The men always bear the burdens on their backs; the women on their heads, their backs usually being pre-occupied by the inevitable baby, for the baby is never left at home. Whether the mother is going to market to sell goods, to church to hear mass, or to a funeral to weep in the procession, the baby always goes too; and, what seemed most strange to us, we never once, in all the time we were there, heard an Indian baby cry. They seem to be born into the world as old as their fathers and mothers. We never saw children laughing and running and playing as our children do; they were always grave and serious, as if they had the burden of years and grave responsibilities resting on their shoulders. Both boys and girls begin to work as soon as they can walk, and never seem to expect or wish for any fun or play as children here do.

We passed through Indian villages like those with which we were already familiar. Half way to Antigua we stopped at a beautiful place where a tolerable breakfast can be obtained. There is a large garden here of rare and beautiful plants and flowers. From this time there was little pleasure to be obtained from the drive; it was very warm, the dust rose in clouds so thick that we could not see even the tails of the mules, and we were almost suffocated. About eleven o'clock we arrived in the ruined city of Antigua, and drove up to the hotel "Comercio," which is kept by natives, a family specially noticeable for their great beauty, the dusky beauty of the tropics.

Antigua is situated in a fertile, well-watered valley, richer and more beautiful than the one in which the present capital is, for that is almost entirely surrounded by deep ravines, so that the water runs off, and the city has to be supplied by means of aqueducts bringing water into fountains.

It is believed by the people that these great ravines would so break the force of an earthquake as to save the present capital from the fate of its predecessor.

At the time of its destruction, Antigua was one of the finest and richest cities in Spanish America, possessing twenty monasteries, one hundred churches, fine public buildings, and over sixty thousand inhabitants. In this vicinity live the most superior tribe of Indians, those who make the finest pottery, do the richest embroidery and most exquisite carving. The city has been partly rebuilt, and many people still live here; but the whole aspect is that of a ruined city. Everywhere are shattered houses, tottering walls, and crumbling churches. The whole has a sad, gloomy aspect, and is the mere ghost of the former queen of this richest and most beautiful portion of Central America.

The ruins of the churches are most interesting, especially that of the largest, the great monastery of the Capuchin monks, a magnificent building, with enormous domes, arches, pillars, and most elaborate ornamentation. The power of the earthquake was well demonstrated in the tumble-down walls, immense cracks, and huge masses precipitated to the ground. Every arch is broken, every capital fallen, every window shattered, every column decayed, and flowers and cactus are growing everywhere. Much of the building has entirely disappeared, its boundary being marked only by a low line of white, but there are countless rooms left, and we wandered about for an hour or more through the dreary, empty spaces. It seemed as if in the vast cloisters the shades of the old friars still lingered, and we could almost hear the monotonous chant which had so many times filled the spacious rooms. Under this spell we were really startled by being suddenly confronted by a priestly form. A second glance revealed, however, only a wax figure in priestly robes — Ignatius, the patron saint of the church; but it was so very lifelike that every one of us had started back at the first glance. In this monastery, severest penance was performed, and unbelievers were most rigorously punished, sometimes roasted over hot coals, or walled up in cells. Many of these cells, having only a small hole at the top to admit a little air and a morsel of bread, are still to be seen, and were pointed out to us by our guide.

After this we visited the church, of San Francisco, a part of which was razed to the ground, but the front was still standing, though much shaken, full of cracks and with headless and limbless images. Much of the adornment, both inside and outside of this church, is very beautiful. At the left is a portion in which worship is still held, and beneath one image representing Christ in the agonies of death were wax models of parts of the body, offered by devotees of the church, who, if they have a disease in any portion of the body, buy these wax representations from the priest and bring them to this image, expecting thus to be miraculously healed. This is one of the old practices of the times before Luther's Reformation.

We were even more interested in our guide than in the ruin, for he was the brightest little black-eyed boy, who showed us all over the vast old monastery with the greatest enthusiasm, talking all the while as fast as he could. Above all else he took especial pride in the bell, which he seemed to think must be the greatest wonder to us. He kept constantly saying, "la campana, la campana," and urging us to go and see. But we were too lazy to climb a step-ladder and mount a crumbling staircase for nothing but the most ordinary bell, so we tried to satisfy him with pretended admiration of it from the solid ground.

Antigua is well worth a visit just for the magnificent view one sees from the Plaza. In this part of the country the mountain chain reaches its greatest height; and as one stands in the centre of the Plaza, his whole view is bounded by these high mountains, most conspicuous among which are the magnificent volcanoes Agua and Fuego (Water and Fire), rising as if from his very feet.

Agua is the most noted volcano of Central America, and the highest peak, being about fourteen thousand feet high. It is one of the most beautiful sights in the world, in shape a perfect cone, the very ideal form of a volcano. Just a little beyond is Fuego, nearly as high, with three peaks, one of which is always smoking. The earthquake which destroyed Antigua, and those which are now felt almost every night in the capital, are attributed to this volcano. Only a few years ago there was an eruption from it, in which several Indian villages were destroyed.

The eruption was attended by severe shocks of earthquake; great stones, weighing tons, were hurled many miles ; and fire, smoke, and lava were emitted.

The view of these volcanoes is so grand and beautiful that in spite of the sad, mournful feeling one must have in visiting this city, he feels entranced and reluctant to go. They fascinate and allure the beholder, so that he feels as if he never wanted to leave them. It seems a pity the capital could not remain here, for what was gained in safety was certainly lost in beauty of situation; but these mighty forces, the relentless sovereigns of the region, decreed otherwise, and Guatemala fled from them, until they appeared but as blue, cloud-like forms in the distance.

A short distance from Antigua is the site of the old city, "Ciudad Vieja," as it is called, the first capital of Guatemala, and also the site of the old Indian temple. To reach it we rode through beautiful avenues of trees, past large, fine estates and extensive fields of cactus, on which the cochineal insect feeds, for this is the great cochineal-producing section. This whole region is exceedingly beautiful.

At the very foot of Agua was the old Indian capital, and at this place Pedro de Alvarado, the lieutenant of Cortez, fought the battles which made him conqueror and governor of Guatemala. Here he encountered most vigorous resistance. It is said that two hundred and thirty-two thousand well-armed Indians went out to meet him; but the superior arms of the Spaniards, and, above all, the terror inspired by the cavalry, were too much for the Indians, who had never seen horses before, and supposed the rider and horse to be one, some frightful supernatural being or apparition. At the end of six days their king was slain, and their subjugation complete. Alvarado razed the Indian temple to the ground, destroyed their capital, and built on its site a Catholic church and a new city for Spain. This was in 1524, but seventeen years after (in 1541) it was completely buried by a flood of mud and water. This flood is usually attributed to a great internal lake in the volcano Agua. The eruption took place at midnight, so not a soul escaped. Alvarado himself happened to be absent from the city; but his palace was destroyed, and his wife perished in it. The only building spared was the church, which then sat on a mound forty feet high. The flood of mud covered the city just to the steps of the church, so that the ground is now level with the sill, where once there was quite an ascent to it. Near by is a tree where the first mass in the country was held by the Spanish army.

Over three hundred years ago this city was buried and it never has been excavated. When it is, doubtless much that is strange and valuable will be discovered, for it was a very rich city, the Spaniards having collected there all the treasure they could lay their hands upon. There it all rests secure, and above it houses are built and fine estates are cultivated. We visited one at the very foot of Agua, where lived a wealthy fair-haired Spaniard, who received us most cordially and politely, seeming to live entirely thoughtless of danger, with a buried city beneath him and a destructive volcano above. We were so near the volcano here that we could plainly see where the side of the crater was blown off in the eruption. The ascent of this volcano is often made. One can go part way on mule-back and then one has to climb. The view from the summit is said to be unsurpassed, and, on looking down into the crater, it is possible to see water below.

The next day, at noon, we said "Adios" to all in the hotel, for no one here ever omits a salutation where there is the least chance of making use of one, and the servants feel deeply grieved if you do not exchange parting words with them. Then we rode away, keeping our eyes fixed as long as possible on the blue majestic forms of Agua and Fuego. When they faded, our enjoyment was gone, and we were again enveloped in dust. We arrived at Guatemala just in time for dinner, and were, on the whole, much pleased with our visit to its ghostly ancestors. This visit was an impressive one, and was once afterwards forcibly called to mind. It was one night when the national band played at the "Cerro del Carmen." An old Moorish church, the oldest in the country, stands on the summit of this hill, and there is a fine view of the city and these distant volcanoes. It was a strange and varied crowd that gathered there to hear the music. There was the President's family, the poor Indian woman selling candy, the Spanish minister in his coach, American and German ladies and gentlemen, the ragged and dirty "ladino," the handsome, dark Spaniard on a gay, prancing horse, and the poor mozo, just resting from his daily burden, — making in all a gay and curious scene. There in the waning day, looking out toward the powers which had already destroyed two capitals of Guatemala, it seemed as if this, too, were only waiting its turn; as if this gay throng, like the old revellers of Pompeii, were doomed to be overwhelmed by the fury of these remorseless forces.

CHAPTER X.

INTERVIEW WITH PRESIDENT AND MRS. BARRIOS.

PRESIDENT BARRIOS was greatly interested in having foreigners come into the country, especially Americans. Coffee, the principal export of the country, was the one subject in which he was most interested, and when he heard that a representative of a large coffee house in the United States was in Guatemala he sent an invitation for us to call at the "Palace," naming the day and hour. My father was then about to make a trip of a few days to Champerico, one of the large shipping ports, and so had to postpone the interview until his return, and just before our departure from Guatemala. A friend of the President went with us to present us and act as interpreter.

At the entrance of the "Palace" or Government building, we were confronted by a guard of soldiers and officers, and, on presenting our card to one of them, were shown inside the court to the waiting-room, where there were already two Spanish gentlemen waiting for an interview. The officers, after presenting our card to the President, returned and said the General was then busy with foreign ministers, but would see us soon, and told the two gentlemen waiting that they would be unable to see the President that day and would have to call again to-morrow. They seemed astonished, and asked if he had not made a mistake and if it was not the Americans who were to call again.

In about half an hour we were shown into the President's room, which was small, and plainly furnished. There were several piles of books on the floor, and great heaps of all kinds of vegetables and fruits.

The President was a fine-looking man, of medium size, perhaps five feet eight or nine inches, and stoutly built; of a dark complexion, with full beard and with an expression of great will power and determination. He was said to be about fifty years old, though he looked younger. He sat half reclining upon a sofa with his hand thrown over the back of it in proximity to two bell knobs, whose use was told us afterwards : one was to call his secretary; the other a sharpshooter, who in an instant of time would stand with a cocked revolver pointed at the head of the suspected visitor. Such precautions Barrios took against assassination. A year before, his life had been attempted by the bursting of a bomb-shell, and since then he had not appeared on the streets without a guard of soldiers.

When we were presented he scrutinized us carefully and extended his hand without rising; but being satisfied, after a glance, of our honest intentions, he then greeted us most cordially, asking at once if we could speak Spanish, as he did not speak English. He was dressed in plain citizen's clothes, and his whole bearing was at once pleasing and indicative of greatness. Seeing us look inquiringly at the heaps of vegetables, he explained that they were gifts from the Indians, brought to show to him their industry. He was very much interested to speak of coffee, — the principal subject of our interview, — he himself being the largest exporter of coffee in the country. Accordingly, we were invited into the courtyard, where he had sample bags of coffee from his different plantations, showing the quality of the present crop, and these he invited us to examine. He owned extensive plantations and was said to export forty thousand bags annually. As a matter of fact, for years, from 'the sale of all coffee in the United States and Europe, he never had a dollar remitted, but invested it in the countries where the coffee was sold. In the courtyard were seventy-five or a hundred Indians from the country, sitting and lying on the ground in the sun, waiting hours and hours and sometimes all day for a chance to pay their respects to him. As soon as he came in sight every Indian rose and took off his hat. Many were satisfied with a mere glance, while others had some trivial complaint to offer. These complaints were often somewhat amusing, but Barrios always listened to them attentively, and with a few words and a pat on the head sent the Indian off perfectly happy. He always saw that the Indians were protected in what rights they did have, and was worshipped by them.

The interview lasted about an hour. At its close the President expressed pleasure in the meeting; invited us to call on his family, and said if there was any favor he could do us in the way of business, or any courtesy he could show us, he should be happy to do so.

We were most favorably impressed with President Barrios, although previous to this interview it had been quite impossible to come to any conclusion, so contradictory and various were the opinions we heard expressed, some declaring him a cruel tyrant, others a great and wise ruler.

The invitation to call on his family we accepted the day before leaving Guatemala. Their house was very large, but not conspicuous, being built exactly like the others, as Spanish architecture seems to admit of little variety. We were met at the door by one of the governesses, who spoke English, and were shown directly to the parlor, which we had a few moments to observe before " La Presidenta" entered. It was handsomely furnished, although ordinary as compared with houses of wealth in our country, but what especially struck us as peculiar was the arrangement of all chairs in two stiff rows, facing each other; but this we learned was truly Spanish, designed to keep the ladies and gentlemen apart, a matter that is duly considered in all Spanish etiquette.

Mrs. Barrios did not keep us long waiting, but

soon entered, accompanied by two of her children, very bright little girls. We were surprised to see a lady so young and fair, although we had heard much of her youth and beauty. The story of her marriage is well known and illustrates Barrios' will and determination. The first time he saw her he determined to make her his wife. She refused again and again, but yielded when he, by harsh measures, brought trouble upon her family. After their marriage they seemed to live happily except for the shadow cast by the fact that his life was constantly in danger. It was said she had not yet recovered from the shock produced by the attempted assassination of the President.

However varied were the opinions entertained in regard to the President, we heard but one expressed in regard to Mrs. Barrios from the time we entered the country until we left it, and that of highest praise. All, from the wealthy foreigner to the lowliest Indian, pronounced her "the loveliest woman in Guatemala."

Mrs. Barrios is very beautiful, tall, and slender, with a fair, almost pale complexion, with black hair and soft black eyes. She wore white and a great profusion of diamonds. She had a sad, almost careworn expression, which seemed strange in a person so young, beautiful, and holding such a high position; but was it any wonder, for she knew, as we did not, what the next day, February 28, would bring forth; she knew as no one else of the proclamation to be issued by the President on the following day, and his great enterprise of "La Union."

She spoke English, as do the children, quite well. She talked of her great love and admiration for the United States, and said the one wish of her life was to see it again, little knowing how soon and under what sad circumstances her wish was to be gratified. She seemed to enter most fully into all her husband's plans for the advancement of Guatemala, and spoke with enthusiasm of all the new enterprises undertaken by him, and especially of the contemplated railroad. With equal enthusiasm she spoke of the education of her children, which seemed one of the greatest interests of her life.

As we were leaving, she expressed regret that the United States was so ignorant of her country, and bade us, on our return, write some articles for the newspapers, "that the people might know there was something besides Indians in Guatemala." She expressed, as did the President, desire to serve in any way possible; and now that she is making her home here, we can only wish that our people will extend to her such courtesy and kindness as were shown to us in her country both by herself and the President.

The next day, the day on which we left Guatemala, Barrios issued his decree proclaiming a Union of the Central American States, and himself "Supreme Military Ruler." Not many weeks after, he was slain in battle, and we heard the news with great regret; for that he had done and would have continued to do a great and good work for Guatemala there can be no doubt. Far be it from us to attempt to judge him. It is almost impossible for any one to do this justly, even though he has been in the country and seen him, opinions and reports were so contradictory and various; for, like all great men (and he was great), he had staunch friends who fairly worshipped him, and bitter enemies who as thoroughly hated him; but one and all alike attested to the fact of the great work he had done for Guatemala, of his ability to rule, and his superiority over any man in Central America. To illustrate, one gentleman, a resident of Central America, who had a son in San Salvador, after railing at Barrios in the strongest terms as a cruel tyrant, went on to say, in the next breath, that Barrios had made the best government in any of the states, and he himself should be glad if Barrios were President of San Salvador, for that government had no stability; there was no basis for business, and titles were not worth the paper on which they were written.

The government of Guatemala is a republic in name merely. The council of state consists of twenty-four members, elected by the house of representatives, consisting of fifty-two members elected by the people. We made inquiries about the elections; but, as far as we could ascertain, there seemed to be no regular method. Ballots are sometimes issued among officials and the principal men, and they vote according to instructions — at least so we are informed. Barrios made the government somewhat more stable; but before his time, as is now the case in South America, there was every little while a fight for the presidency, the victorious party holding it until some faction rose up which was strong enough to overpower them.

Barrios became ruler of Guatemala by force, as is the manner in all these republics. He placed himself at the head of a small band collected on the borders of Mexico, and took possession of the government. He was by title President, but in reality absolute monarch. All the laws were instituted by him, and not by the legislature of the people. At one time a new member took occasion in a speech to oppose a certain measure, but he soon after disappeared, and was never again seen, neither did the legislative body ever dare inquire what had become of him. There was a perfect system of spies throughout the country; every official was watched, and every sign of a revolution was suppressed in its incipiency. At one time a party of conspirators hid themselves in an underground passage in one of the old monasteries of Antigua. It was a long time before they were found; but when they were, Barrios had them all shot. When, later, his life was attempted by the bursting of a bomb-shell, he pardoned the executors, but shot five or six who were suspected to have planned the deed, and banished others, one of whom was an intimate friend, the next highest in position in Guatemala, one of the ministers, and the owner of the finest estate which we saw in the city. Barrios scrupled at no means to be rid of any one who stood in his way, and that his acts were often most cruel there can be no denying, but it must be further granted that he doubtless thought them necessary in order to rule the people and establish a stable quiet government. Furthermore, much as it is and ought to be condemned, it must be remembered that this is the Spanish way of doing business. They clinch all their acts with a sword or pistol, and think there is no force or power save in the use of these weapons.

Of the last act of his life we can but say it was unfortunate. He professed to be truly patriotic. Certainly that the Central American States should be united under one government was and is most desirable. Then they might be something of a power, while now each by itself is insignificant. There was but one man in Central America capable of standing at the head, and that was Barrios. A union had been greatly agitated, and throughout the country all professed to desire it, though, as the end showed, they did not really wish it. There is too much petty jealousy between the different states to make it possible in this generation.

His skill in planning the movement was certainly admirable. Not the slightest suspicion of it was known the day beforehand. We heard one or two remarks which we called to mind afterward, though they did not impress us at the time. Some little curiosity was expressed as to why so many soldiers were going to Guatemala, and it was said that President Barrios must be "up to something." The answer always was, "It is only a review of the troops. He is expected soon to cross the country, and all preparations are being made for him." This was most remote from his real plan.

The greatest excitement was caused by the proclamation of the Central American Union, and enthusiasm ran high. The newspapers afterward received from there were full of articles most patriotic, eloquent, and stirring. There were some which would hold rank with the finest expressions of patriotism ever uttered in any country or in behalf of the noblest cause. Nothing is easier than to excite these people of imaginative, impulsive mind to the highest degree either of frenzy or nobleness, and in this case they were thoroughly aroused.

The treachery of Zaldivar, a lifelong friend of Barrios, to whom he was indebted for the presidency of San Salvador, put an entirely new aspect on affairs, and was a great and unexpected blow to Barrios, who then went down to subjugate Salvador. At first, Guatemala was successful, but in the battle of Chalchuapa Barrios was slain while rallying his men, and with his life all inspiration and courage died out. There was nothing left to inspire the army, though they fought most bravely for his dead body, and rescued it only with the loss of many of the bravest and best sons of Guatemala.

A letter lately received from there pays the highest tribute to the action of our American minister, Mr. Hall, through the whole trouble. He worked nobly and well, and was the one "mainstay" in all the commotion, his house being a refuge not only for Americans, but also for many natives whose lives were in danger, especially after the death of Barrios, when all was disorganization and tumult. He did much toward stopping the trouble, and, if Zaldivar had not intercepted the cablegrams from Washington to Guatemala, would probably have averted war altogether, as Barrios waited nineteen days to hear from Washington before beginning proceedings, such was his respect for the judgment of the United States.

In these days the good old Latin proverb, so worthy of consideration, seems to be forgotten, "*De mortuis nil nisi bonum*" (of the dead nothing but good). There has been much written about Barrios, both favorable and unfavorable, principally the latter; but the great mistake all are liable to make in estimating his character is to judge him by the standard of our day and country, forgetting that he was one of and ruled over a semi-civilized people, over a nation for three hundred years under the grinding and deteriorating rule of the Spaniards, and still really belonging to the centuries far in the past. Look at the condition of all colonies of Spain, those who have thrown off the yoke and those still under its power! They are marked by constant insurrections, by deeds of violence, by instability, corruption, and stagnation. Such was Guatemala when President Barrios became ruler, and for it, everything considered, he accomplished wonders. He was without doubt the man for the time and place.

What he did can perhaps be no better expressed than by an extract from a Guatemala newspaper, translated from the Spanish, to the truth of which all must testify:—

"General Barrios reformed completely Guatemala. From a half-savage people he made a body of free citizens, educating them in innumerable schools, which he founded even in the insignificant little villages, and giving them the rights of franchise. The rule of horror and death, of times not far distant, was replaced by good laws; freedom of worship and of the press were, thanks to him, effected in Guatemala. He has left many works of unquestionable merit and practical utility; he crossed the republic with lines of telegraph, built the railroad in the South and planned one in the North, established lines of horse-cars in the capital, and built many public buildings, such as the hippodrome, the penitentiary, the post-office, the polytechnic school, hospitals, and many more, too numerous to mention. Above all, he created a spirit of action and enterprise which, if it was not completely dead, was sunk in heaviest lethargy very like death. He found nothing and created everything, and such a work must be that of a great genius — a genius that gave life and action to everything touched by his hand."

The article closes with a high tribute to his memory, which we would add, not as expressing a universal sentiment, but that of his admirers. "A noble great man, General Barrios died for his people as he had lived for them. The ball that passed through his heart smote also Guatemala. Now, since science and love are powerless to restore the life in an instant of time taken from the dear ones who mourn his death, and for whom he gave his life's blood, let us, by making every effort to maintain public tranquillity, honor the repose of the illustrious commander, whose life was a constant struggle and perpetual effort for the good and advancement of Guatemala. May his sleep be respected, and let us go on with determination and faith to work earnestly for the prosperity and aggrandizement of Guatemala, thus realizing the dearest dream of the heroic soldier, able statesman, and honored President, General J. Rufino Barrios."

CHAPTER XI.

COFFEE PLANTATIONS, GROWTH AND CULTIVATION.

THERE is not a more beautiful sight than a coffee plantation, with its shrubs of rich dark green, bearing white fragrant blossoms and bright crimson berries; and the visitor to Guatemala, whether specially interested in coffee or not, will be sure to visit one after another of these fine estates. They usually cover many acres; have good buildings, fine avenues of trees, and large gardens nicely laid out, containing beautiful and often rare plants and shrubs. The owners are generally wealthy men, either Spaniards or Germans, and always receive visitors with the greatest pleasure and cordiality, showing them all about the estates and sending them away loaded with flowers.

The plantations cover acres of ground, and the land is perfectly cultivated, — not a weed or spear of grass is allowed. The coffee plants are set out at equal distances, and in rows on a perfect line;

all of them are of uniform size and height, and the tops look as perfect as a hedge that has been trimmed with the greatest of care. The average crop of a plantation is about one thousand to fifteen hundred quintals annually. One plantation near the port of Champerico exports fifteen thousand bags and has three hundred and eighty thousand trees.

The coffee plant is a shrub growing to the height of twelve to fifteen feet in its wild state, but under cultivation is kept down to six or eight feet. The shrub has a single stem, opening out at the top into long, dense, drooping branches, which fall to the ground, making an unusually beautiful looking plant. The leaves are long and pointed, and of a dark, rich, glossy green. The flowers come out from the angle of the leaf in groups of from four to twelve, and are small, white, and fragrant, resembling the jessamine. The fruit succeeds the blossom, and very much resembles a cranberry in color, form, and size. When ripe the berries are of a dark crimson color, and consist of a pulpy mass containing two oval seeds, which are convex on one side and flat on the other, and lie together face to face, separated only by a thin skin or parchment. Sometimes only one seed forms, and in process of growth, as it pushes itself against the dividing membrane and encounters no opposing growth, it naturally rounds over and makes the small, round bean known as pea-berry.

To secure the proper growth of the coffee, plenty of shade is required. To reach this result on some plantations, the plants are set out several feet apart, and between them are planted shade trees which grow to a great height, with the foliage on the very top. On other plantations banana trees are planted in like manner for the same purpose. When these rules are not followed the coffee plants are placed very close together, and when fully grown the tops meet, making a solid body of very dark foliage, shutting out every ray of sun from the ground.

The conditions for the cultivation of coffee in Guatemala are very much unlike many other coffee-growing countries; a very large part of the coffee grown in Guatemala is on table-lands, or high plains, at an elevation of four thousand feet or more, and the varieties of soil are very marked, varying from a deep rich black loam to a red clay or sandy soil;

all of which are sometimes to be found in one or two miles; consequently, in order to purchase Guatemala coffee, and get a high standard and uniform quality, every condition of growth and preparation must be known to the buyer.

These conditions are, the proper elevation, location, the particular kind of soil, the planter's manner of cultivation, facilities for curing, and proper machinery. One single condition left out of the many is almost sure to produce a coffee that will be below the standard of a fine drinking coffee.

Most of the planters are rich, and have complete machinery. Large planters have the latest improved and best machinery, with power, usually steam. The works are quite extensive, and always located as near as possible in the centre of a plantation. If a running stream of water can be obtained in such a location, it is of great benefit; for plenty of water saves labor and makes a more "stylish" coffee.

The berries are picked and carried to the factory, where they are run through a pulping machine, a stream of water passing through the hopper with the berries. The machine breaks the pulp, separates the berry, and the pulp is carried off and spread around the trees for dressing. The coffee berry runs off in a spout into a reservoir, which has a cemented bottom enclosed by masonry, — a cemented wall about two feet high, making it water-tight; water is run through with the coffee bean, when it is washed; the water is then drawn off, and the coffee remaining is dried in the sun; it is then put through a machine which breaks the skin, winnows it, and makes it perfectly clean from chaff and dirt; the coffee is next all hand-picked, or graded, making some four qualities; then it is bagged, and when sold transported to a railroad or shipping port by carts or on the backs of Indians. The labor is done by the Indians, the men working the land, the women and girls doing all the work at the mills, and picking the berries. In parts of the country where there is little coffee culture the berry is pulped by the Indian women by hand. The coffee is then dried and sold "in parchment"; that is, after it is pulped and dried, the berry remains encased in a thin membranous skin, then it is transported to some town where there is a factory, where it is perfected for market. Labor is very cheap; the price for men per day is one real (12½ cents), for women a medio (6¼ cents).

The coffee of San Salvador is cured without water, and it has a dark, dingy, discolored appearance; much unlike the first quality of Guatemala, which is clear, waxy, transparent, and of a green color.

It is claimed by merchants and planters in Salvador that coffee cured without water (which method is compulsory with them, as they have no water during the coffee season) is better, as it retains all the strength and flavor, which the use of water extracts to a certain degree; but this theory, in our opinion, is not correct.

The term "washed coffee," as understood with us here, is coffee that has been washed after it has been once dried and milled, which, apparently, does extract some of the strength and flavor, and consequently lessens the value of coffees naturally fine and rich, so far as the drinking quality is concerned, while the same process used on coffees which are rank and harsh in flavor is beneficial. But the use of water in pulping, while the bean is green, soft, and full of moisture, thereby cleaning and curing, but retaining the original color, must be the perfect way of curing, as this preserves the natural, perfect flavor of the berry.

The curing of coffee is of vital importance, as it is in this that the foundation is laid for fine quality, aroma and perfection of style; and when coffee, by improper treatment, becomes stained, spotted, or discolored, the drinking qualities and green appearance have certainly been proportionally damaged.

Guatemala coffees have a wide range of value in drinking merits, although the style and appearance of the bean may be about the same, and this difference of drinking quality may often occur in the same coffee-growing district. The bulk of the crop of Guatemala coffee is exported to London and Hamburg, little coming to the United States, and that being third and fourth quality. San José and Champerico are the shipping ports of Guatemala, Champerico being very much the larger port; and the quality of the coffee grown in this vicinity is said to be the finest in the country.

The facilities possessed by Guatemala for producing fine, "sightly," perfect coffee are not excelled by any coffee-growing country; but there are immense obstacles to be overcome in purchasing coffee in Guatemala. As before said, the conditions already described must be studied to know the value of the coffee one is purchasing. Besides, only a very small part of the coffee is purchasable at all, as many of the large plantations are owned by parties in Europe, to whom the coffee is all shipped; and most of the planters that are able to move their crop prefer to consign their goods to their own correspondents and take their chances with the markets. This class of planters will not sell their coffees except at a fabulous price. What is more strange, there is never a bag of coffee in any city or shipping port for sale; neither can a sample be found. The purchasable coffee is found only at the plantation, where the whole crop must be bought "in parchment," or an advance of cash made to enable the planter to have the coffee milled and graded; bags must also be furnished him, and money to transport to the shipping port.

Such are a part of the obstacles to be overcome in purchasing coffee in that country, which makes it a hazardous business for a foreigner.

CHAPTER XII.

CHARACTER AND CUSTOMS OF THE PEOPLE.

The population of Guatemala is given as one million four hundred thousand, but the census is not very exact, and probably there are a million and a half of people. Of these nearly a million (950,000) are Indians, three hundred thousand "ladinos," and about one hundred and eighty thousand whites, including Spaniards and foreigners.

The characteristics of the Indians have already been described, but we wish to add something about their origin. There are twenty different tribes, each with its own language; but all save three or four belong to the same family, the general name of the Indians of Guatemala being that of "Quiche."

They trace their origin through a long line of kings back to the ancient Toltecs, who formerly inhabited Mexico, the majority of whom were driven out by the coming of the Aztecs in the eleventh century. These Toltecs are supposed to have been the most superior race of Indians that ever inhabited this continent. They possessed a wonderful civilization, and all the finest architectural remains and ruins in the country (those of Yucatan and some parts of Mexico) are attributed to this race. When the Aztecs came, the Toltecs, not being a warlike people, offered no resistance, but some of them moved further south, while a part remained, became amalgamated with the Aztecs, and taught them their wonderful civilization — that civilization which so astonished Cortez and his army when they entered Mexico, and remains of which are still to be seen in the city at this day. Unlike the Aztecs, their history is not stained by the offerings of human sacrifice on the altars of their gods, nor by the horrible practice of cannibalism. To the traveller it is most interesting to note how the present Indian tribes and the other inhabitants of Guatemala differ from those of Mexico. But of this we shall speak later on. Morelet, the naturalist, who has given greatest study to these "Quiche" Indians, describes them as "an active, courageous race, whose heads never grow gray, persevering in their industry, skilful in almost every department of art, good workers in iron and the precious metals, generally well dressed, neat in person, with a firm step and independent bearing, and altogether constituting a class of citizens who only require to be better educated to rise equal to the best."

Their condition has already been shown. It seemed to us, as near as we could determine, very much like that of the serfs in the old feudal system. We were told that if a man bought a piece of ground the Indians on that land were bound to work for him. Roads are built and repaired, aqueducts made, and the government coffee plantations all carried on by "forced labor," the poor Indians working without a cent of pay. As we have shown, they do the hardest work for the smallest pay, and have but few rights. They have the power to choose, subject to the approval of the "Jefe," one of their number as "alcalde," a sort of judge, to whom they appeal for protection and justice. This is their only voice in the government.

The "ladinos," especially the lower class, are inferior to the Indians in cleanliness, honesty, and industry. Still, they regard themselves as infinitely superior, and treat the Indians with great contempt.

The dress of the people is characteristic. That of the Indians has been described. In and about the capital it is somewhat different from that of the interior, in that the women, instead of wearing a loose skirt, take a straight piece of cloth and wind it tightly about them, with an awkward effect. One tribe near Antigua dresses in black. The women of the lower class wear an embroidered chemise, a full skirt, and a bright colored "rebosa" (a single shawl), over the shoulders and head, as they never wear hats. Of the higher classes, the wealthiest have adopted the European dress; and often the costumes are imported from Paris, and are very elegant. Very few use hats, but they wear very gracefully the Spanish mantilla upon their heads, and the black shawl of fine texture over the shoulders. It is said that "when the ladies put on hats they leave off smoking." These varied costumes, so different from ours, make the streets a gay and novel scene to the traveller.

All the people, whether of Spanish or mixed

blood, are truly Spanish in their customs and manner of life.

Boys and girls are placed in separate schools, even in their youngest years, and girls are most carefully watched and secluded. The streets are full of Indian women, but one sees very few of the higher classes, and this was so noticeable that we asked, "Where are the ladies of Guatemala?" and received the answer, "In their houses." It is contrary to custom and all rules of etiquette for a lady to go on the street alone, even in the daytime. She must be attended by a servant or another companion, and it is improper for ladies, even in groups of two or three, to be out after dark unattended by a servant. Ladies and gentlemen never walk together on the street unless married.

An American girl does not half appreciate her freedom and independence until she goes to one of these countries. Indeed, the American and German ladies have found these customs so tiresome and disagreeable that they have rather broken over them, and now if a stranger walks the street unattended she is forgiven by the people, who have learned that the customs of other nations are different from their own.

The young ladies being kept so secluded by the Spanish custom, love-making must necessarily conform to circumstances; and the suitor, since he is not allowed admission into the presence of his inamorata, frequents the pavement in front of her house, and gazes up at her balcony, where she sits ensconced behind the bars. This performance is called in Mexico "hacer el oso" (playing the bear), and in Spain "pelando la pava" (plucking the turkey). It is often continued for months, and even years, without success, the result depending upon the will of the parents, who, after a time, make inquiries into the young man's prospects, and, if the results are satisfactory, invite him into the house, although they never allow him to see the young lady alone.

Naturally, the young people make the most of every meeting at the theatre, opera, and Plaza, where, by motions and glances, they carry on most extensive and ridiculous "flirtations." The Mexicans especially, as every traveller will observe, indulge in this folly to the greatest degree.

Spanish gentlemen consider it complimentary to stare at a lady, and will even put their heads into a carriage where one is sitting, and gaze at her steadily for several minutes. American ladies of blond complexion travelling in these countries get so much admiration of this nature that it is exceedingly disagreeable, and even painful. Blue eyes and light hair are so rare that they are greatly admired, and boys will often stand and look up into a lady's face for some time, and pour forth a constant stream of compliments, which, if she understands Spanish, is truly overpowering.

These customs strike an American as very peculiar, and make him exclaim, "Consistency, thou art a jewel," for there is a great show of virtue and little of the reality. The whole Spanish system of society gives plainest evidence of its falsity, and the fact that it defeats its own purpose. The words of Lara, in "The Spanish Student," regarding the lack of virtue among Spanish women, are often repeated in Guatemala and Mexico.

That the moral state of society is low, there can be no doubt. Most deplorable of all is the existence of evils similar to those in the South during the times of slavery. That the Indian women are not lacking in virtue, however, is proved by the fact that many beautiful Indian maidens appeal to their "Jefe" for the protection of the law against the wealthy planters.

Gambling and drinking, especially the former, are carried to excess. We saw much less drunkenness in all the time we were away than can be seen in one week in the city of Boston. But gambling exists to an alarming extent, although no more among the natives than among the foreign population. Poker is the favorite game; playing cards without money is never thought of; whist parties, composed of both ladies and gentlemen, meet regularly Sunday nights to play "con dinero" (for money).

In Guatemala, as in all these countries, Sunday is the great holiday. The market is then most crowded; the stores most largely patronized; the best plays are presented at the Opera; and the bull fight occurs. There are very few, even among the Americans, who observe the Sabbath after they have been there a while.

It is surprising how soon Germans and Americans fall into the ways of the country, giving as their excuse a phrase we heard until we were heartily disgusted, "Hay la costumbre en Centro

America" ("It is the custom in Central America"), as if with a change of climate it were necessary to change one's sense of propriety, and even one's ideas of right and wrong.

The prevalence of smoking has been alluded to. It sounds rather peculiar, but is no uncommon question to ask a lady if she smokes, and many foreign ladies, both young and old, adopt the practice, although we are happy to say we saw no American ladies who smoked.

One of the most hopeless features in regard to the state of society there is this lack of a sense of responsibility on the part of foreigners, both Americans and Germans. They are a superior race, who have had better advantages, and are so looked upon by the people; but instead of doing anything to elevate the country, the majority of them simply adopt its vices and then condemn the people for the same sins.

Our personal experience with the people was so pleasant that we dislike to think at all of their faults. We met many truly good people, whose kindness impressed us more than the wickedness of the greater number, and makes us feel well disposed toward the whole. Travel across the country as we did, and partake of their hospitality, and remember their origin and history, and you will love them in spite of their wickedness. But if you want to be convinced of the doctrine of total depravity, get some of the foreign residents of Guatemala to talking about the natives. They will grant them no excellences whatever. They will tell you the people are false, deceitful, treacherous, and desperately wicked; that they are polite and say kind things without meaning a word of it, simply to flatter you and make you pleased with yourself and them; and that they never do a kindness save from a selfish motive. We could not believe this, and on mentioning one and another, even all of the natives with whom we had any dealings, we were always assured that these were indeed most excellent and thoroughly good men. Was it, then, that we met only exceptions? If so, we are glad, and we know at least there were some as good and true as live in any part of the world.

Two characteristics of the people (most trying to all who deal with them) are certainly to be condemned. These are their indolence and dilatoriness. They are slow and lazy, as a rule, and will never do to-day what can be put off until to-morrow. They lack the energy and enterprise so characteristic of Americans. But then, again, we could well learn from them both patience and amiability. They did seem the most patient, amiable people in the world. We never saw a person among them in an ill humor, never heard any cross words, or witnessed a single quarrel. Americans might learn much, too, from this simple, warm-hearted people in politeness, courtesy, and hospitality, for as compared with them we are cold, stiff, formal, and selfish.

They have many little expressions of salutation and leave-taking, and forms of compliment, which have no equivalents in English, but which are very pretty and very pleasing to the traveller who knows a little of the language. You can but feel more kindly disposed toward the bright, black-eyed young fellow who takes care of your room, when he greets you every morning in a pleasant way with "buenos dias," and on bringing you your candle at night says, "duerme bien" ("sleep well"), or "pasa buena noche"; and you cannot feel half as irritated over a poor bargain at one of the stores when the clerk politely bows you out with an "adios."

If Spanish politeness is false and hollow we did not find it out. If kind words were said without meaning, simply to make us pleased with the speaker, the result was surely accomplished, and we felt more kindly disposed toward the whole of Guatemala for the pleasant words spoken in that musical language. Many acts of real kindness and self-sacrifice we know were extended us from the pure good will of the people; if any were done from a selfish motive, it is no more than we meet with every day at home. From our personal experience with the people from first to last, we can but speak with affection and gratitude of all.

The history of Guatemala may be given in a few words. Conquered in 1524 by the Spaniards, it was under their rule until 1821, when it threw off the yoke; and now it celebrates that occasion on September 15 of every year, as we do the 4th of July. It was then annexed to the Mexican empire under Iturbide, but in 1823 became a part of the Central American Federal Republic. This union did not last very long, and Guatemala, after being conquered by San Salvador, finally defeated the Hondurians and Salvadorians, and established its independence under Carrera in 1851. Since then its development has been retarded by petty wars, by the destruction of many villages and cities by earthquake, and by revolutions. The Liberal party came into power in 1870. The archbishop and the Jesuits were driven into exile, and when Barrios became President, in 1872, the order was declared extinct and its property confiscated. His work has already been described. Barillas succeeded him as President.

CHAPTER XIII.

GUATEMALA TO PANAMA.

THE area of Guatemala is estimated at from forty to over fifty thousand square miles. An accurate statement is impossible, because the boundaries are not settled and surveys are few and imperfect. It is divided into twenty departments, each of which has a "jefe politico" (governor).

Its mountainous character has already many times been mentioned. The range is a part of the Andes and affords magnificent and varied scenery, being always clad in verdure, and having beautiful terraces, many mountain streams and waterfalls, enormous ravines and precipices of the wildest description. The number of volcanoes is very great, estimated at thirty-one, of which at least five are active. The most famous and highest, Agua, fourteen thousand feet high, one of the most beautiful cones in the world, has already been described.

So much of the land being elevated, the climate is very agreeable and healthful, save in the hot, moist coast-lands, where malaria lurks and seizes every visitor who lingers.

Guatemala is very rich in resources, which as yet have been very little developed. Many of the strata are metalliferous, though few mines are worked. Silver, lead, coal, and marble are found, and the Spaniards obtained, during their rule, forty million pesos (dollars) of silver in Chiquimula, where mines are still worked, though with poorer results.

Many valuable woods are found, there being upwards of one hundred kinds of timber trees. The other chief products are coffee, — now the most important, gradually superseding that of cochineal, formerly the greatest product, — maize, frijoles, rice, wheat, indigo, cocoa, sarsaparilla, tobacco, sugar, vanilla, chili, and many fruits. The great need is capitalists to develop the country and make use of its wonderful natural advantages and resources. Those who have already come are principally Germans, and that they are making money there is no doubt.

The lack of facilities for travelling is the first

great obstacle to be overcome in the development of the country.

We heard of but two railroads, that from Guatemala City to San José, a distance of ninety miles; and one from Champerico a short distance into the interior. The roads are mostly narrow paths, very few suitable for carriages, very bad even in the dry season, and in the rainy, almost impassable. Bridges are few, and generally in poor condition. But there is steady advance in this direction; much was done during Barrios' administration. It must be remembered there are many obstacles to overcome, the great mountains and huge ravines. It seemed to us, as we traversed the mountains in the last of the way to Guatemala, that it would never be possible to have anything but that narrow path; still, afterward, when we saw what engineering had accomplished from Vera Cruz to Mexico, it seemed that a railroad might be possible even here. Should there ever be one from Panzos to Guatemala City by the route which we took, a most wonderful and beautiful journey would be open to the tourist. There could hardly be a more interesting trip to one liking to depart from the great highways of travel and see man in his primitive condition and nature in her own magnificence and beauty; but at present the hardships to be endured will prevent all, save a very few, from ever going, and will detract from the pleasure of those who have the courage to venture.

Having passed two weeks in the capital very pleasantly, we were ready to continue our journey. From here only ninety miles remained to complete the trip across the entire republic of Guatemala, from the Atlantic to the Pacific side, and this last portion, much to our relief, we were enabled to accomplish by rail.

The morning of our departure many of the friends we had made during our stay were at the station to see us off, and it was with real regret that we parted with them and with the city, where we had spent many pleasant days.

The train started at 8 A. M., reaching San José at about 2 P. M. The road is descending all the way from the elevation of Guatemala, over four thousand feet, to the level of the sea, and the grade is so steep that for most of the way no power is used and even then it is necessary to put on the brakes. The ride is for the most part uninteresting, relieved only by the views of the mountains and the beautiful Lake Amatitlan, and by crowds gathered at every station, the ever-interesting Indians selling fruits and "dulce" (sweets). As we came down from the height we suffered exceedingly from the heat and dust, which made the journey so unpleasant that we began to think it was not possible to travel comfortably, under any circumstances, in this country. Here we had occasion to observe another Spanish custom, that of the gentlemen all smoking in the cars in the presence of the ladies, there being no smoking-car on the train.

The port of San José is the usual small Indian town. The Pacific Mail Steamship Company has an agent living there, an American, with whom we had previously become acquainted, and at whose house we spent a few hours before taking the steamer. There is no harbor at San José; it is simply a "roadstead." Indeed this coast is notable for its lack of harbors, and is regarded by navigators as very dangerous. The mighty ocean has full sweep and offers one of the grandest exhibitions of its power in the raging tumultuous surf with which it breaks upon the shore.

There is nothing at any of our beaches at all comparable with the tremendous surf we saw at San José. Huge waves, mountains high, white and foaming, broke on the beach with a deafening roar and such awful power and fury as to make one shrink from the thought of launching upon its waters. A long iron pier has been built far out into the water beyond the greatest force of the breakers, but steamers are not able to come even to the end of that, and are obliged to anchor two miles from shore. Landing passengers over such a raging sea is both difficult and dangerous, and sometimes in a storm the water is so rough that steamers refuse to receive or land passengers, and oblige those on board to go on to the end of the voyage, and take their chances of landing on the return trip.

Soon after our arrival in San José, the captain of the steamer on which we were to sail sent word for passengers to come on board early, as the sea was very rough that afternoon. Before we reached the steamer we had to undergo a series of novel experiences; novel even to us, after all we had passed through. On the pier we were beset by a numerous crowd of boys claiming a "real" apiece for bringing our baggage from the cars to the pier. After we had paid more boys than we had pieces of baggage, they still kept appearing, each claiming he had carried this or that, and all looking so much alike, with their dark faces, that it was impossible for us to recognize the ones we had engaged. We were disposing of our last "reales," and all the small boys in San Jose were getting rich, when the agent's wife, well acquainted with these urchins, interposed in our behalf and sent them off. Then our baggage was weighed and we were charged the exorbitant sum of five dollars and fifty cents for the privilege of crossing the iron pier.

The next performance was as unique as it was unpleasant. At the end of the pier was a large iron cage attached to a system of pulleys. In this cage the passengers, five or six at a time, were let down from the pier into a large flat-bottomed boat loaded with coffee. I must say I shrank from the transit, and we waited to be the last. As soon as we were fairly seated and had grasped the iron bars, the machinery moved with a dismal grating sound, the men on the pier gave the cage a push and down it went into the bobbing boat below. The process of being lowered was quite a quick one, but the sensation when the cage was swung off the wharf, out over the raging sea, was not at all pleasant. The launch into which we were lowered was rocking so that we had to make great haste to be seated, and were glad to cling to the baggage so as not to fall overboard. In this coffee launch, with the rays of the hot sun pouring down upon our heads, we were obliged to sit, tossed up and down by the billows, until a tugboat came and towed us out to the steamer. The poor tug had a hard struggle with the foaming billows, and was tossed about like a chip, sometimes riding the crest of a great wave, and then entirely disappearing in the trough of the sea. It went first to the right, then to the left, and staggered like a drunken man, but finally brought us safely to the steamer. Even at this distance from shore, where the steamer was anchored, the waves were too rough for it to be safe for passengers to mount the steps; so a barrel was lowered into the launch, and in this, one at a time, we were pulled up into the steamer.

Once on board and fairly out of Guatemala, we felt the truth of Mrs. Stowe's saying, "The pleasure in travelling is to *have* travelled," and now, while we think of that country with affectionate interest, we can but say our pleasure in seeing Guatemala is to *have* seen it ; and, should we ever go there again, we should take the Pacific Mail from New York and content ourselves with a visit to the capital and vicinity, the most interesting part of the republic.

The journey across the country, with all its strange, odd, and interesting experiences, will live always in our memory, and form part of our waking and sleeping dreams. It was a mixture of bitter and sweet, of which the former impressed us most then, the latter now. It is an experience we would not part with for "the wealth of Ormus or of Ind." It is one we would not repeat for twice that sum.

The steamer *San José*, on which we were embarked, was one of the Pacific Mail Line, sailing from San Francisco to the Isthmus. It was a fine large steamer, perfect in every respect, and we fully appreciated its excellences.

There were not many passengers, and very few who spoke English. I was the only lady. Two of the passengers in particular attracted our attention, a French priest, and his companion and servant, a young boy of Guatemala. The priest was a queer, wiry, sharp-featured man who was bound to be first in everything. He was just ahead of us in buying his ticket, and we had to wait a good part of half an hour while he counted out his fare and the boy's in "real" (12½-cent) pieces. When we were about to get on to the steamer from the launch, he pressed forward in eagerness to be ahead. The captain shouted, "Let the lady come first"; but he didn't understand English, and jumped into the barrel as soon as it was lowered. For some reason he was very anxious to make the acquaintance of my father, and would obtain a few English words from a German who talked with him, that he might be able to make a little conversation. That he was sincere in his calling we could not doubt, and for that respected him. He read his prayer-book hour after hour, and was most faithful in his devotions. The boy who attended him was, like most of the boys of Guatemala, very interesting, with the characteristic traits of the people, bright, quiet, docile, and very devoted to the old priest, who kept him studying French and the prayer-book all day.

This boy's ignorance of the world was surprising, as we chanced to find out; for, while the priest was once absent a few minutes, we took occasion to try to divert him with papers and books. He was pleased with the pictures, but regarded them in a very different light from what we expected; for on seeing a picture of Lydia Pinkham he looked very reverent, and asked if it was not sacred. To him pictures of women were representations of saints and angels to be worshipped, and he will never know they can represent simply inventors of patent medicines.

We sailed in the evening, and one night brought us to La Libertad, a port of San Salvador. Here the steamer stopped all day loading coffee, and it was very hot.

The next day we were in sight of three republics, San Salvador, Honduras, and Nicaragua. All along this coast there are volcanoes; one in San Salvador, named Izalco, has an eruption every fifteen minutes.

The water was smooth and beautiful all day; and it was delightful sailing, except for the heat, which was the greatest we had yet experienced. That night there was a "norther," and the wind howled furiously and the great ship rocked and creaked fearfully for a few hours. These "northers" blow several months during the year, and are the great dread of all navigators; not that they are really so dangerous if the ship is kept out from the land, but the wind is so cold as to almost chill the blood in one's veins, and so powerful that the ship can make scarcely an inch of progress, and is only tossed about at the mercy of the gale in a vain battle against wind and wave.

The next day the ocean was as smooth as a lake; we passed Costa Rica, and were near land. We had a most gorgeous sunset, and a full moon at night; besides, the water was all aglow with brilliant phosphorescence, which looked like great fiery serpents playing about the steamer.

Wednesday we sailed south of the Isthmus, along the mountainous shore of Colombia; for in order to get into the Bay of Panama it is necessary to go several hundred miles along the coast of South America. It was a lonely, mountainous, rocky shore, though rather strange and interesting.

Thursday, at 9 A.M., we were in the Bay of Panama and at the end of our voyage, but had to wait until afternoon for a tug to come after us and take us ashore. The bay is very pretty and contained much shipping; there were many dredgers at·work, dredging for De Lesseps' canal.

Our whole voyage had been the perfection of sailing. The Pacific had demonstrated the appropriateness of its name, "peaceful," and had been as smooth as possible on the whole passage, save the one night of the "norther." The weather was perfect, we had most brilliant sunsets, and a full moon every night; hence the Pacific Ocean will always be associated most pleasantly in our minds. The steamer was a fine one, the fare good, and the captain a pleasant, dignified gentleman and an agreeable companion.

CHAPTER XIV.

PANAMA, ASPINWALL, AND THE ISTHMUS.

AFTER leaving Guatemala, our plan was to visit Punta Arenas, in Costa Rica, where my father wished to inspect the coffee crop; from there we purposed to go to the Isthmus, and thence to Vera Cruz, by the first route which should present itself.

As it happened, the *San José* did not stop at Punta Arenas, as we had at first expected. This, however, was no great disappointment to us, for we knew exactly what the place must be — a hot, unhealthy Indian town, where we might be obliged to stay several weeks before getting passage in any steamer. But coffee was the one great object of this journey; my father's zeal was so great (and mine had become as great as his), that we should have endured without complaining all the discomforts of this coast town, had we been obliged to stop there.

On arriving at the Isthmus, we were greatly rejoiced to learn that a steamer was advertised to sail the next day from Aspinwall, the other side of the Isthmus, to New Orleans. From the accounts we heard of the unhealthiness of the Isthmus we were anxious to get away from it as soon as possible, and that we should thus arrive just in time for the steamer was, as we afterward found, a matter of the greatest good fortune.

Surely the hand of Providence guided us all the way through this journey, and made "all things work together for good." The manner in which we had made connections, in a country where travellers are often delayed weeks, and even months, was truly wonderful. From the time we left New Orleans, we had not been able to plan definitely any further than from one point to another, yet we had spent just the amount of time we wished in each place, and had experienced but few and short delays. Every one who knew of our journey across Guatemala said it had been accomplished with an expedition unprecedented. Then, to crown all, we were not obliged to linger in the unhealthy Isthmus, a possibility we had feared.

The unhealthiness of the Isthmus can scarcely be exaggerated. The yellow and the Chagres fevers reign supreme; men die like dogs in the street, and no attention is paid to them. Travellers have been known to go on shore in perfect health and die before the next morning. We were told that any day one could see fifty fresh graves in the cemetery.

The place was full of Frenchmen, engaged in the work of the canal, and this addition to the population greatly increased the unhealthiness. There is no attention whatever paid to drainage, neither are there any sanitary regulations. When the tide is out the hot sun beats down on the flats, and a miasma like a cloud rises, bringing malaria and death.

Passengers on the Pacific Mail steamers are not allowed to go on shore even for a night, but are always kept on board until the steamer is ready to sail from the other side of the Isthmus, no matter how long that may be.

As our steamer was advertised to sail at noon the next day, we were obliged to spend one night on shore, and were strongly advised to stay in Panama as preferable to Aspinwall.

We arrived in the bay in the morning; but, as before stated, the steamer was obliged to anchor out from land, and we had to wait until afternoon for the tug to take us over to Panama. We found it a most wretched place. The streets were narrow; the houses were old and dilapidated; and the air was hot, and laden with disease.

We went at once to the "Grand Central" hotel, the best in the place — a new building, but already beginning to look old, for the climate in a short time ruins everything. It was situated on one side of the Plaza, opposite an old crumbling cathedral. There was a most terrible odor pervading the whole house, exactly like that of a decaying corpse, and very likely it was; for next morning we read in one of the papers of a half-decomposed dead body being found under one of the hotels. We could neither eat nor sleep, and felt as if in a charnel-house.

After passing a wretched night, we took the train at seven o'clock in the morning to cross the Isthmus. It is only a three hours' ride, but the fare is twenty-five dollars in American gold; that is, for a foreigner, — a native goes for ten dollars.

There was no place we ever found that was such a perfect Jew shop as the Isthmus. If one escapes the fever and ague, the people do their best to get all his money away from him. We had been warned of this, and instructed by the captain what prices to pay, but could never seem to carry out our friend's advice. For instance, he told us just what sum to give for a carriage to take us to the train, telling us to ask no questions of the driver, but offer him the proper amount without a word. We did so, whereupon the fellow demanded more; and when we explained that was the usual fare, he had the audacity to tell us that we had to pay more because we were Americans.

The ride across the Isthmus disclosed to us a miserable country,—hot, swampy, unhealthy. There were frequent stations, but they were only wretched little negro villages, and all along the way were numerous graveyards and fresh graves; for the soil, composed of decaying vegetation, breathes out death as soon as overturned by the spade.

In building the railroad, it has been said that every sleeper cost a man's life; and without doubt as many if not more lives will be sacrificed in the digging of the canal.

Everywhere work on the canal was visible; but there seemed little connection between the different portions of the work, and nothing like more than a mere beginning. We were told by one of the engineers that so far only the "installation" was done, only ten million of the required two hundred and fifty million cubic metres of earth had yet been removed. The undertaking is a vast one, far exceeding that of the Suez canal, and every one there believed it would not be finished for many years.

At ten o'clock we arrived in Aspinwall, or, as it is always called there, Colon, this being the real name of the place, given by the people in honor of Columbus; Aspinwall is the name given by the Americans, but is not used on the Isthmus.

It is quite impossible to say which place is the worse, Colon or Panama. Everybody in Panama said, "It is not healthy here, to be sure, but not nearly as bad as Colon"; and in Colon they all said, "It is much healthier here than in Panama." From our own experience we concluded that both places were as bad as they could be.

One cause for the great mortality in both places is the excessive intemperance. Nowhere is temperance more necessary, and nowhere is it practised less. There is great mortality among the French, because they indulge so freely in wine. Sailors drink as soon as they get on shore, and consequently many of them die before they ever get back to the ship. Many of the Americans coming here start for a saloon as soon as they land, almost invariably come down with yellow fever, and frequently die in a few hours. A native of South America — like all these people, far from a total abstainer — added his testimony to the necessity of temperance in these countries where there is yellow fever. He said if any one would be strictly temperate he could with perfect safety go through a place where an epidemic of yellow fever was raging, and that he himself never took the least quantity of intoxicating drinks when in a region where the disease was prevailing.

We found Colon a most wretched place; hot, dirty, and producing the same ghastly impression as did Panama. The railway station in which we were obliged to wait, was merely a baggage-room, without a single chair, and was full of Jamaica negroes, as rough and lawless a set of beings as can be found.

Supposing we had but two hours before the sailing of the steamer, we hastened to make the necessary arrangements, but were greatly perplexed in not being able to find any one with whom we needed to confer, as they were all sick with chills and fever. The steamer was not in dock; the agent not to be found; and the American consul, who had letters for us, was likewise missing. We met with obstacles everywhere, and had infinite trouble.

Furthermore, as we learned afterwards, the place was in such a turbulent state from a rebellion which was just beginning, that it was not safe to be on the streets, and our lives were in constant danger.

Finally, we learned that the steamer would not be ready to sail for a day or two, but that all the passages were even then engaged. The prospect was most disheartening, for the thought of staying on shore another night at one of the hotels was appalling. There was a feeling of death and danger in the very atmosphere; and although I was perfectly well, and had no fear for myself, I was alarmed for my father, for he had been very ill three days in our voyage on the Pacific, and the night before, in Panama, had been very sick again.

We both began to feel very discouraged. We had slept in mud huts, in the open air, lived on Indian fare, and encountered many hardships cheerfully; but now for the first and only time (although neither of us acknowledged it until we got home) we felt like giving up, and almost wished we had never undertaken this journey.

Finally we decided to get our baggage down to the wharf, and see if we could not get on board the steamer, for once on the water we should feel perfectly safe. As we walked through the wretched streets to the wharf, I thought of the fine Pacific Mail steamer to sail that night for New York, and said:—

"Father, let us take the Pacific Mail steamer and go home."

"Do you want to give up Mexico?" he answered; and, perceiving by a few words that he was firm, I said no more.

We reached the wharf just as the steamer came into dock. My father, in his eagerness, climbed over a big post, with more agility than I could have supposed possible, and was on board the steamer before she had fairly landed. As I anxiously awaited the result, the words I heard from the captain sounded like a knell:—

"All first-class passages engaged. Your baggage can be put on, but we are not ready for passengers until to-morrow."

But, feeling that this was our only refuge, my father used all the persuasion and eloquence of which he was capable, to induce the captain to take us. He was reluctant to do so, because he had not suitable accommodations for us; but my father declared we would eat anything, and sleep on deck if necessary. Finally he said:—

"There stands my daughter on the wharf, and I believe we shall both die before morning if we have to stay on shore."

This appeal was effective, and the captain consented to take us, saying:—

"You may come on board as soon as the plank is put out."

We were not long in getting ourselves and baggage on to that steamer; and when we had our chairs placed on deck, we felt quite content, not caring whether we had a place to sleep, or anything to eat, so long as we were out of Colon.

Our experience in the Isthmus was certainly the most dangerous and trying one we had. I felt, as I sat on the deck of the steamer, like one who had passed through a fiery furnace unscathed. The words of the ninety-first Psalm, in this, as in all the other trying moments of the journey, were a veritable reality:—

"A thousand shall fall at thy side, and ten thousand at thy right hand; but it shall not come nigh thee."

CHAPTER XV.

VOYAGE IN AN ENGLISH STEAMER.

THE steamer in which we were to take our second passage across the Gulf was an English steamer from Liverpool — the *Legislator*, of the Harrison line — very large, and carrying much freight, but with accommodations for only a limited number of passengers.

As the steamer could not sail for a day or two, we were the only passengers on board. That night we dined with the purser and the first and second officers, who were very pleasant and agreeable, and excited our wonder and admiration to think they could laugh and joke while anchored at Colon.

After dinner we had a conversation with the captain, whom we found to be a most intellectual, cultured, kind and thoughtful gentleman, with much of the humorous element, which made him a still more agreeable companion. From him we learned more of the wretched condition of Colon, and of the many annoyances suffered there by himself and officers. They had been waiting two days to get into dock, their berth being occupied by a French steamer, and had yet all their cargo to discharge, although it was then the day for them to sail. They had brought a company of fifty soldiers to aid the government in the rebellion. These soldiers had nearly exhausted their supply of provisions, and it was almost impossible to obtain anything eatable in Colon. The captain himself was just recovering from a severe illness occasioned by being on shore but a few hours to transact necessary business.

We began to realize then how great an act of kindness had been done in taking us on board, and felt most truly grateful. The captain's experience in getting a doctor very well illustrates the lawless and dangerous state of affairs then existing. Being alarmed at his condition, two of his officers went on shore for a physician, but had not proceeded far when they were arrested, and they were only saved from imprisonment by presenting a letter showing that the steamer had just brought soldiers to aid the government, and was therefore entitled to protection. After further trouble a doctor was found, but he absolutely refused to go without a guard of soldiers to conduct him. These were finally obtained, attended him to the steamer, waited until he had seen the captain, and then conducted him back again. He considered such precautions absolutely necessary for the protection of his life.

It is very dangerous to be in any of these countries during a revolution, and we began to feel that we had been very fortunate in encountering no harm, and in being able thus to escape from the country before the worst. What the place must have been after the rebellion fairly set in, can scarcely be imagined! We left none too soon.

The second day, Saturday, in the afternoon, the steamer sailed, and we never felt so happy to leave any place as we did to leave Colon. It seemed strange that any one would try to live in the Isthmus; but men will risk their lives for the "filthy lucre," and this place offers great inducements.

The passengers were an interesting and a miscellaneous company. There was one Mexican, several Spaniards, two Frenchmen, three or four Americans, and two Venezuelans; but Spanish was the language spoken throughout the voyage. The majority of the passengers were from the Isthmus, and were thin, yellow, and sickly looking victims of chills and fever, or half eaten up with quinine. They were very wealthy, and were going to visit the Exposition, or to travel in the United States.

In about an hour or two after starting, the steamer began to pitch some, and, with the exception of ourselves and one other passenger, everybody on board was sea-sick. Though it was not very rough, they were a most dejected company for several days, their susceptibility being due, without doubt, to the fact that they had been living in Colon and had been so long without a breath of pure air; or it also may have been partly due to the fact that many of them were Spaniards, of whom it is said this liability to sea-sickness is a general infirmity. Certainly in this mixed company of passengers the natives of Spain seemed to suffer the most.

Among the passengers was the editor of the Panama *Star and Herald*, an excellent paper, in three languages — English, French, and Spanish. With him were his wife, baby, and nurse. They furnished considerable diversion for all of us, — especially the baby, an odd little thing not much more than a year old, but very bright and lively. She looked like the rest who lived in Colon, and reminded one of Victor Hugo's description, "A bit of clay containing a spark," but a bright spark it was, and shone merrily out of those little black eyes set in the tiny round yellow face. She was not sea-sick, and consequently not quiet. She went everywhere; and was found sometimes in the pantry, sometimes in the kitchen, and even once succeeded in confiscating a bunch of raisins; a thing which would have required more skill than any adult passenger possessed, for the ship was a most intricate place in which to find one's way. One night we had a great gale, and the captain, coming through the saloon at midnight, found, much to his astonishment, this same baby promenading about all alone.

Among the passengers was the Dutch consul of Panama, the son of the Spanish consul, a wealthy Mexican who spent his time in travelling, a very interesting young married lady of New Orleans, whose husband, a cultured Englishman, was one of the superintendents of the works at the Isthmus; and a brother and sister, natives of South America, though the brother was then a resident of New York. These two had been having a very serious time. They started from New York to go to Venezuela, the brother to accompany his sister. Arriving at the Isthmus they found their country in such a state of revolution that the port was closed, and they could not enter. Then they were obliged to remain in the Isthmus some three weeks, until the arrival of this steamer, by which they were going to New Orleans to wait until a cessation of the troubles.

Such was the miscellaneous company on board, and any student of human nature could find ample scope for all his powers, and sufficient amusement and entertainment from his observations.

The second day, Sunday, there was even more motion than on the first. All the passengers were on deck, and, as the captain said, were "all anchored," for everybody sat perfectly quiet in an easy-chair, a deathly silence reigned all day, not a sound was heard or a movement made, save when some poor victim visited the rail and paid the necessary "tribute to Neptune."

The next day was smoother, and some of the passengers even ventured to go to the table; but in the night there was a gale of wind, and they were all sick again. That night was a wretched one for us. We tried, with several others, sleeping on deck in our chairs, thinking it would be better than the crowded cabin, but the wind howled furiously, making frightful and unearthly sounds in the rigging; the ship rocked terribly, and snapped and groaned as if coming to pieces. We got but a few snatches of sleep, and that was disturbed by nightmares and frightful dreams. Next morning we were all a dilapidated looking company, and we did not recover from the effects of "the blow" until afternoon.

From that time we had fine weather; but we were constantly haunted by fears of a "norther," for at that season a voyage across the Gulf could scarcely be made without encountering one.

Thursday the wind changed and blew warm from the south. The sea was as smooth as glass, and it was so very warm that even the inhabitants of Colon were languishing from the heat. This had a meaning for the captain, and he said: "There's a 'norther' blowing somewhere; this is one of the premonitions, one of its twenty-four-hour warnings." And again in the evening he said, "We shall get the 'norther' before midnight, but are so far up the Gulf, and so under cover of land, that its fury will be broken." It was all as he had said. The "norther" came at eleven o'clock, and with it a thunder shower. There was creaking, and cracking, and raging enough; but the great steamer hardly rocked, and rode steadily in spite of the elements. There was little sleep for any of us, and none at all for the faithful captain.

It was this night that he found the baby taking her solitary promenade in the saloon.

One very important and most useful member of the steamer's crew must not be overlooked. That was George, the second steward, a fair-haired English boy, of eighteen, whose office it was to bring the meals on deck to those unable to appear in the dining-room. In fact, he seemed the most useful and essential part of the whole ship; for, if anything whatsoever was wanted, all we had to do was simply to call, "George," and he appeared as if by magic to do our bidding. It was a mystery where his retreat was; certainly out of sight, but not out of hearing. During the "sea-sick" period he was in constant demand, and even the baby, not a whit behind her elders, learned to go to the head of the stairs whence he appeared, and call, "Georgie."

Two other objects of great interest to us were the "stowaways," two urchins from the streets of Liverpool, who had tucked themselves away so carefully in the great ship before she sailed as to escape the vigilance of the officers when the usual search was made after their kind. They were very curious, interesting specimens, with such odd faces! One had a big, round, fat face, all out of proportion to the rest of his body; the other had gray hair and a very old face, as the captain said, "a face that might have been knocking about forty years ago, instead of belonging to a boy of eleven or twelve."

When found these boys were set to work for their passage, and the little fellows did well. They used to bring all the food on to the table from the kitchen, and in order to get into the dining-room had to come up the stairs on deck, where we could see them; and it was one of the greatest diversions of the voyage to watch them as they came up through the hole carrying their great platters and covered dishes with ever the same unchanging, expressionless faces, like two little machines. We could not help wondering what their fate would be, thus early cast upon the world to make their own way, without help or sympathy from any one. Only this was certain: no very great or happy lot lay before them.

One of the chief characteristics of the voyage was the frequent appearance of "the flowing bowl." On recovering from sea-sickness the men resumed their usual custom, and five or six times a day passed around champagne, sherry, or a "cocktail" of some description. It was brought up in a large soup-tureen, poured into glasses with a soup-ladle, and served to all on deck.

The entirely different way in which this drinking was regarded by two of the lady passengers furnished an admirable illustration of the influence of birth, education, and surroundings, upon a person's belief and conduct. One of the ladies was a New England girl, brought up under the shadow of the Maine law, and a thorough advocate of its principles. This constant drinking was to her very painful, and she firmly refused every glass, from first to last.

In direct contrast, as representing the other extreme of the temperance question, was the young lady from South America, a handsome young girl, who drank every time with the gentlemen, and on a plea of sea-sickness called for glasses of brandy and water besides.

Without arguing from effect to cause we can certainly conclude the inefficacy of liquors in cases of sea-sickness, for the advocate of temperance was not sick at all worth mentioning, and was, until the very last meals, the only lady at the table, while the patron of brandy and water was terribly sick the whole passage, and even when the water was calm and smooth could by no means be persuaded to leave her reclining-chair, in which she sat day and night during the whole voyage.

It is often said, and generally granted, that in travelling in countries where the custom in regard to this matter is so different from ours, it is absolutely necessary to drink wine. This is not true. It is sometimes unpleasant at first to refuse, but the one who does conscientiously will never regret it, and will lose nothing of the respect and esteem of his fellow-men.

Quite an amusing incident happened at dinner one day. We had English plum pudding, and the captain ordered some sherry put into the sauce; then happening to look at the New England girl, he laughed, and said, "George, capture some of that sauce before the sherry is in." George said, "All right, sir," and dashed like lightning for the door, for he had many a time passed her sherry in vain. Returning he gave the verdict, "Too late, sir." But she did not on this account refuse her favorite dessert, the most delectable of all puddings, a genuine English plum, made by an English cook.

We should have reached New Orleans Thursday, but the currents had proved unfavorable and the "norther" had delayed us. Friday morning we had arrived at the mouth of the Mississippi, and there was a long and vigorous whistling for a pilot. At eight we were at the quarantine station and had a visit from the doctor, every person, crew and passengers, passing in review before him. All day we sailed on the Mississippi, but it was not at all pretty, as there was very little verdure save the orange groves. At six o'clock we reached New Orleans and the voyage was over.

We had been on the water five days and a half; all the passengers were most eager for the shore and hastened off as soon as the steamer landed; but we were in no such haste to desert our refuge from Colon, and were the last to leave. The conduct of our fellow-passengers was most entertaining, especially the way in which they arrayed themselves in their most gorgeous apparel before going on shore. Some of the transformations were wonderful, for these people from wretched Colon and off to " Los Estados Unidos" for a good time were in just the right condition to delight in dressing up like children. We stayed calmly behind and watched this hurried landing till all had gone; first the passengers rushed pell-mell, then the officers went, then the crew, and finally even the two little kittens strolled out, and after them the two little stowaways.

We must pronounce this voyage of all the four we made in this winter trip the most interesting. Others were taken in finer steamers, with better accommodations; but none were more really enjoyable. Much of this, if not all, was due to the great kindness and thoughtfulness of the captain. Throughout the voyage he was ever mindful of the comfort and welfare of each one, and together with the purser was constantly trying in every way possible to make the voyage a pleasant one. The passengers were all duly grateful, and to show their gratitude, on the occasion of their last dinner together, presented him with a written testimonial setting forth this appreciation of himself and his officers.

CHAPTER XVI.

ACROSS THE GULF TO VERA CRUZ.

ARRIVING in New Orleans we were a little disappointed to learn that a steamer sailed for Vera Cruz in three days, which would give us but little time for the Exposition or rest from our sea voyage. One whole half day had to be given to searching for a lodging place, as every hotel was full. Finally we succeeded in getting two rooms, and for our meals went to the French restaurants, where we found the cooking most delicious, and had a perfect feast of good things.

All the time we had we spent at the Exposition, which we found inferior to the Centennial. The chief features were the Mexican exhibit and the government building, both of which were very fine.

The thought of crossing the treacherous Gulf for the third time, and of landing in pestilential Vera Cruz, was not very pleasing, and, as if to keep it ever before our minds, we were continually being presented with hand-bills urging us, in the largest type and strongest terms, to "see the Gulf of Mexico without fail before returning home." If those who heeded this solicitation saw anything worth seeing in the Gulf of Mexico we are glad, for it is about the last place in the world to which we should go for pleasure.

There are several lines of steamers from New Orleans to Vera Cruz. We heard greatest praise of the Mexican line recently established, and should have been glad to have patronized it could we have made connections; but it was then the last of March, and every day was bringing us nearer to the time of the yellow-fever epidemic, and consequently making it more and more dangerous to visit Vera Cruz.

We sailed on the steamer *Whitney*, of the Morgan Line, from Morgan City, eighty miles from New Orleans. The steamer was a very good one, with excellent accommodations for passengers, and first-class fare. As it happened, the Gulf was in a very happy mood, smiling on us every day almost as placid as a lake; but we did not love it, for all that, nor forget our first experience on its dreary waters.

The passengers were nearly all Americans, going to Mexico for business or pleasure, and, on the whole, they were more companionable than those of our previous voyages. Still, in spite of the fine weather and people who spoke English, we did not really enjoy the voyage, for we were tired of the water, of the long, monotonous days at sea, of being so long out of sight of land, and of having nothing to do save to watch a few flying-fish or an occasional flock of sea-cranes.

As usual, our greatest amusement and diversion was in studying our fellow-passengers; but having in the preceding chapter disclosed to view the associates of one voyage, we will forbear in this, and merely mention as some of the principal a charming French lady, an artist, who captivated everybody; a company of Catholic "Sisters," among whom was the lady superior, teacher of President Diaz' children; an elderly lady, of imposing mien, chaperoning her daughter and two young men about to settle as physicians in Mexico; and a gentleman and his mother from Chicago, who became our friends and constant companions all the time we were in Mexico.

Truly, if "the proper study of mankind is

man," it is also the most interesting, and we found one of the greatest enjoyments in travelling to be this opportunity of meeting and making the acquaintance of so many different people.

Sailing Tuesday morning, we arrived in Vera Cruz Saturday morning, making but one port on the way, that of Galveston, where we stopped long enough to go on shore and see something of the city.

The entrance into Vera Cruz is exceedingly dangerous, and shipwrecks are frequent. It is impossible for any but small boats to land in a "norther," and if one happens to be blowing on nearing Vera Cruz, the steamer is obliged to put back to sea and wait until it is over, which is sometimes as long as three days.

As at all the ports on the Central American and Mexican coasts the steamer anchors out from land and passengers go on shore in small boats, so that the first introduction a stranger has to the country is to a motley crowd of dark, ragged boatmen. These men throng the steamer immediately on its arrival, and behave in all respects like importunate hackmen, augmenting the confusion by a constant stream of Spanish, until one has a perfect conception of the tower of Babel, and does not fully recover from his bewilderment, nor feel quite sure whether he has engaged passage of one, a dozen, or in fact of anybody at all, until he and his baggage are settled in the boat and really sailing for shore.

Having several times previously passed through these scenes, we were a little better off than many of our fellow-passengers, to whom it was a first experience.

Vera Cruz! How shall we describe it? A queer old place, as strange as any in the world, and yet on our own continent. Founded by Cortez in 1519, the first spot in Mexico on which the Spanish army landed, it was the starting-point of their great and marvellous march and conquest, and, later on, the port through which went untold wealth to enrich the kingdom of Spain.

The view of the city from the water is very pretty, on account of its castles and shining domes and spires, its strange architecture, its waving palms and fruit trees.

But most prominent of all is the castle of San Juan de Ulua on an island half a mile from shore, where the Spaniards found, when they first landed, idols and evidences of human sacrifices. The castle was begun in 1662 but not finished until 1796. It was a very strong fortress and the last point relinquished by the Spaniards, being held by them four years after the rest of the country was given up.

Now it is used as a prison for political offenders, and terrible is the lot of all incarcerated there, for the cells are dark, damp, and filthy, and some are nearly filled with water. It is said that among other poor wretches there is one so long deprived of air, light, and freedom that he has lost nearly all intelligence, and has even forgotten his own name.

What stories those walls might reveal, even as terrible as the prison of Chillon, whose description accords very well with this castle :—

> "A double dungeon wall and wave
> Have made — and like a living grave."

We tried very hard to find out which was the best of the three hotels in Vera Cruz, but invariably received the answer, "Whichever one you go to, you will wish you had gone to some other," so we finally decided on the "Vera Cruzano," because we happened to meet a clerk from there speaking

English. Our rooms were comfortable enough, though with stone floors and single iron bedsteads, but we could not eat the food. The cooking was Spanish, and everything was spoiled with oil, red pepper, or some vile sauce, so that with a bill of fare that in writing would almost compare with that of Fifth Avenue Hotel, we really went hungry, subsisting almost solely upon a cup of coffee or chocolate and "pan dulce," the only articles of food we could enjoy.

The balconies and corridors were made pretty by many plants and beautiful singing birds, among which was one most remarkable parrot, which chattered all day in Spanish, and sang songs, blew the trumpet, or played the cornet in a highly entertaining manner.

The houses of Vera Cruz are built in the Spanish style — of small stones covered with plaster and tinted, but they are higher than those of Guatemala. The city is well supplied with horse-cars, and by taking one marked "Circuito" we saw the whole place in a short time. A strange place it is, and in no respect a pleasing one, the Plaza being its only attraction.

The city has a very old and oriental aspect; and

one might easily imagine himself in ruined Pompeii from glimpses into the interior of some of the courtyards of the old houses. The street scenes are indeed strange and curious; the Mexicans in their striking costumes, with broad sombreros; the Indians with their burdens; the hundreds of turkey-buzzards constituting the board of health (for the drainage is surface); the packs of "burros," poor, thin, wretched little donkeys, carrying great loads of charcoal, "zacate," or barrels of water; and another curious turnout, also common in the West Indies, that of three mules harnessed side by side, with the driver riding on the back of one of the mules instead of sitting in the wagon.

The population is rather mixed, and impressed us most unfavorably. All the bad that has been said about Mexicans and Spaniards we could easily believe when we walked on the street and looked into the villanous faces of those we met — faces enough to make one shudder, whereon the word desperado was plainly written.

One day we witnessed a strange sight. A large, powerful man of this class, bound with stout ropes and surrounded by a guard of heavy-armed soldiers, was being led through the streets. On inquiry, a friend said this man so carefully guarded was one of the bandits, and that two or three a day were brought in from the country, where they had' been captured by picked men, appointed by the government to search them out. These bandits have no trial, but are despatched by the favorite Mexican method — shot dead without judge or jury.

Coming, as we did, from Central America, we were most forcibly impressed with the difference between the natives of Guatemala and those of Vera Cruz, and our thoughts turned back with affection to the common but kind-hearted and amiable people of the former place.

The unhealthiness of Vera Cruz is well known. There is probably no time during the year in which it is free from cases of yellow fever. The middle of April a quarantine is put on, and from May to November the disease rages fearfully, there being fifteen, twenty, and even thirty and forty deaths a day. The months of December, January, and February are safest, because coldest; since the disease does not exist in a temperature of seventy-five degrees or less. We were in the city the last of March, and there were cases of the fever, but we had no fear, for we saw no appearance of any danger, and could scarcely believe the stories we heard of the unhealthiness of the place; besides, had we not been in Panama and Colon, places we believe to be far worse than Vera Cruz, although it has earned the name of "la ciudad de los muertos" (the city of the dead)? It seemed strange that there should be ten thousand inhabitants in such a pestilential city, but it is a rich port, and besides it is possible to have yellow fever and live; and those who have it once do not have it again. A German representing one of the most prominent houses there, a resident for fifty years, who, with his family, had had the disease, jokingly pronounced it a comfortable one. "You have no pain," he said, "and in ten days are well or dead."

Most of the deaths are among the Indians who come in from the country, for, thinly clad and sleeping out of doors, they are drenched by the rains and soon die of the fever. The epidemic rages most during the rainy season, and the greatest care must be taken not to get wet, for then a chill follows, and just as certainly the dread fever.

The way to treat the disease is to go immediately

to bed, wrap up warmly, and keep in a perspiration for ten days, taking no solid food whatever (for that is sure death), and only hot herb-drinks to keep up the perspiration. An American, who survived the fever by carrying out this treatment, said that at the end of this time he looked as if he had been parboiled, but it was the only way to escape death.

No one cares to stop in Vera Cruz, yet all arriving by steamer are obliged to stay one night, for the train for Mexico leaves only in the morning. Our fellow-passengers all left the day after arriving, but we stayed longer, because Vera Cruz was a very important port for the shipment of coffee.

The first day the heat was excessive, the greatest we experienced in all our journey, and we felt quite prostrated; but the next day a north wind sprung up and it was quite comfortable.

On the third day of our sojourn in Vera Cruz, hastily drawing business to a close, we decided to start next morning for Mexico, and packed our trunks with joy at the thought, for on leaving Vera Cruz we left behind all business, all hardships, and all danger from pestilence, and started on a real pleasure trip to the City of Mexico.

CHAPTER XVII.

A DAY'S JOURNEY FROM COAST TO CAPITAL.

THE distance from Vera Cruz to the City of Mexico is one hundred and ninety miles. It is traversed by a railroad, which is one of the finest pieces of engineering in the world, and reveals to the traveller most magnificent scenery, crossing, as it does, the high range of the Eastern Cordilleras, tunnelling through mountains, bridging over great chasms, and running along the brink of precipices thousands of feet deep. There were almost insuperable obstacles to be overcome in the construction of this road over a high range of mountains. It was sixteen years in building, not being opened throughout its entire length until 1873, and the cost was thirty-nine million dollars. Almost all the stock is owned in England, hence it is called the "English road."

The scenery is especially remarkable from the fact that one passes in a few hours from the level of the sea to an elevation of over eight thousand feet, and sees the vegetation of all zones, from the palms and hot-house flowers of the coast, through groves and plantations of oranges, bananas, coffee, and tobacco, to the corn and wheat fields of our own clime, thence to the pines, oaks, and evergreens of colder latitudes, even to within sight of snow-peaked Orizaba. "In no country in the world can you pass so rapidly from zone to zone, — from the blazing shores of the heated tropics to the region of perpetual winter, from the land of the palm and vine to that of the pine and lichen; for in twenty-four hours this can be accomplished, and the traveller may ascend a snow peak with the sands of the shore still upon his shoes."

On the morning of our departure for the City of Mexico we rose early, and before light passed out of the "Vera Cruzano" as the servants, sleeping on cots by the doorway, were just arousing themselves for their day's work. One of them followed us and solicited patronage, saying it was hardly safe for us to go unattended at that early hour. The streets were silent and deserted, and we decided to be relieved of our bundles and accept him as an escort. He conducted us to a restaurant, where he waited upon us himself, bringing us our morning cup of coffee and "pan dulce," then accompanied us to the station, found us seats on the left-hand side of the car, where we could get the finest views, and then took leave of us very politely, as if we were old friends. For all this very acceptable service he charged but five cents!

We mention this because among all the discomforts of travelling in these countries there are some conveniences which we do not have at home, and one of these is the abundance of servants to be met with everywhere, who will carry your bundles any distance and render most willing and efficient attendance for this paltry sum of five cents. It is their sole business, and they are quite happy if they get one job a day.

The cars are marked first, second, and third class — the latter being occupied by Indians. We were early, and found we had some time to wait, but the car soon filled with people, nearly all Americans, who arrived the night before by steamer from New York. Some Mexicans who were parting with each other gave us opportunity to observe the Spanish custom of leave-taking, which seemed to us most peculiar. The men clasped each other in an affectionate embrace and pressed either cheek; the ladies adopted the same method, with the addition of a kiss.

The train starts at six o'clock, and for a while runs along the hot, dusty plains of Vera Cruz, but soon begins to ascend, and vegetation becomes more luxuriant, with orchids, roses, bananas, pine-apples; olive, lime, and orange trees; curious air-plants, and a tangle of flowering vines. As the way grows steeper, to overcome the obstacles presented by the hills the road has to wind in and out and over great "barrancas" (ravines), at whose base rush mountain streams. It crosses several bridges, one quite famous, that of Atoyac, three hundred and thirty feet long, where the traveller gets a view of one of the most exquisite cascades, tumbling over the rocks of a wild ravine, clad in richest verdure. Occasionally one sees huts of the natives — rude structures made of poles, with thatched roofs, as in Guatemala; and the train stops at one or two small stations, crowded with Indians, who have fruits to sell.

Our fellow-passengers, almost from the start, had all been looking through glasses for a glimpse of Orizaba, a volcano seventeen thousand three hundred and seventy-eight feet high, with its foot in the land of perpetual summer and its head in a region of lasting cold.

We looked in vain at first, but after a while, chancing to glance to the right, suddenly we beheld this most magnificent spectacle, Orizaba, with its crown of dazzling snow glistening in the sunshine. The sight was finer than we could ever have imagined. It was at once very grand and very beautiful, and an exclamation of wonder and delight involuntarily escaped us at this first and unexpected view of a snow-capped mountain.

The first station of importance is Cordova, which is situated in a rich valley at a height of two thousand seven hundred and three feet. It contains fine orange groves and large sugar plantations, and is the centre of a coffee-growing district.

Soon after leaving this station the road for a time runs along the brink of the wonderful "barranca" Metlac, which is one thousand feet deep, and then it crosses the chasm by a bridge commanding a fine view. The road, always ascending, winds in and out, dashing through dark tunnels, crossing bridges over deep ravines, or curving around a bend of the mountains. These curves are often so sharp that from one's seat in the car the whole train is visible from one end to the other, and the winding road itself can be seen traversing the mountains by a sinuous path, like the trail of a serpent.

The fact of the ascent is plainly shown by the change in the character of the vegetation; for our familiar cornfields begin to appear mingling with plantations of tobacco, coffee, rice, and sugarcane.

This is one of the most fertile valleys of Mexico, and to our fellow-passengers just from the United States — which they had left in cold, bleak, and dreary March — the sight of it was like a first vision of the Garden of Eden; to us it was like a second and better view, for in our journey across Guatemala we had scenery like this, only we now saw it under more auspicious circumstances, a railway car being a far better observatory than a mule's back.

At half-past ten we reached the city of Orizaba, at an elevation of 4088 feet, having in the last sixteen miles climbed 1375 feet! Here we stopped long enough for breakfast, and were glad to find it quite eatable, the cooking being more American than that of Vera Cruz. The city is ancient, and very pretty, with a picturesque situation and quite healthful climate. It is a health resort for Vera Cruz during its scourges of yellow fever.

Leaving Orizaba, the road still ascends, and in the next three hours climbs three thousand feet! The country now grows less fertile, but the scenery more sublime. Having passed the noted gorge known as Infiernillo, or Little Hell, a giddy and terrible precipice, we were all shut in by mountains, and could see the winding track below and above us. Looking up we saw a faint line far, far above, on the very top of the mountain, and said to each other, "Can it be possible that we are to ascend to that height?" It was indeed possible, but not to an ordinary locomotive. The one employed is the powerful Fairlie "double-ender," which looks like two engines combined. This giant literally began to climb the mountain, like a fly crawling up a wall. Slowly it crept up the steep ascent, occasionally stopping as if exhausted, and being recuperated with a supply of wood and water. Thus with almost breathless anxiety we ascended to the region of the pine and oak, and to a height greater than that of Mt. Washington. Suddenly a most glorious panorama was spread out before us — a fertile valley, thousands of feet below, all shut in by mountains, and called most appropriately "La Joya," the Jewel. In the centre of it is the village of Maltrata, laid out in perfect squares of living green, with streets as straight as an arrow, and with picturesque houses and flowering gardens, the whole effect being so beautiful that it did not seem like a real town, designed as a habitation for mortals, but like the work of some fairy for enchantment. The scenery at this point was the finest in all the journey, glorious beyond description. As the train wound in and out, we had one moment a full view of this beautiful valley, then turning a bend of the mountain lost it altogether; but again and again, when we thought we had seen it for the last time, it burst upon our view in all its beauty. The passengers were all excitement — one moment on their feet, uttering exclamations of surprise and wonder; the next, spell-bound, and almost breathless, at the magnificence and awfulness of the scene. The track, like the mule-path of Guatemala, is for ten miles built along the mountain side, on a bed of terraced rock, with a grade rising more than four feet in every hundred. Once the track crosses a bridge over a chasm ninety feet long, where, if anything should happen, the train would be precipitated two or three thousand feet.

We were all aware of the dangerous height we were scaling, for Maltrata looked scarcely larger than a toy village; and a mule train visible half-way up the mountain looked no larger than so many mice. The grandeur of the scene was too great to be long enjoyable, and we drew a sigh of relief as we reached "La Boca del Monte" (the mouth of the mountain), 7,900 feet above the sea — the end of the steep ascent, and the beginning of the great Mexican plateau. "In the last thirteen miles we had climbed over three thousand perpendicular feet!"

A few miles more of gradual ascent, and at half-past one we reached Esperanza, the highest point, 8,303 feet. Here a long stop is made, and an excellent meal served, but having breakfasted at Orizaba, we spent our time in viewing the station, and the crowd there gathered. As usual, there were many Indians offering for sale various kinds of fruits (many of which are unknown to Americans), and all sorts of sweets and native eatables with which to tempt the Mexican taste, and the curiosity of strangers. But the most noticeable of all the crowd was a handsome looking young Mexican, in a riding suit, presenting an appearance elegant enough to make our greatest "swells" green with envy. With a rich dark complexion, a fine form, and manly bearing, his natural beauty was further enhanced by his dress, which was most elegant and showy, and consisted of a sombrero of drab felt, with an enormously wide brim and a rich trimming of silver; a jacket and vest of spotless white, elaborately embroidered; and trousers of fine black cloth, with rows of silver buttons on the seam from top to bottom. An enormous pistol, and a display of jewelry, completed his elegant toilet, and enhanced the fine appearance of which he was fully conscious, as well as of the admiration which he excited. Then there were three armed soldiers, to protect the train from robbery, for we were travelling in a land of thieves and cut-throats, and every station on the road is guarded by picked men, appointed by the government. The business of these men is to scour the country, search out bandits, and bring them to justice, or, rather, to death, for they are shot as soon as apprehended. This method has proved quite effectual, and so many have been disposed of in this summary manner that for a year there has been no train-wrecking on this road. Before this vigorous policy was adopted, attacks were frequent, and the train rarely went to Mexico with a whole pane of glass in its windows, because of great stones thrown into the cars, and a passenger seldom arrived with all his possessions. On the train there is a guard of thirty soldiers, to protect it from any attack. Every Mexican carries arms, and considers a pistol as much a part of his dress as our men do a necktie. All this array of military power to ensure our safety in travelling, even by rail, did not impress us very favorably with Mexico. In strong contrast to this, and with grateful remembrance, we think of our journey across Guatemala, when, with only a guide and one Indian, wholly unarmed and unprotected, we travelled through the lonely interior of that country in perfect safety.

Our journey from this point was across the dusty table-lands. Here we met the train from Mexico, and parted with our giant "Janus," which must go down the steep descent back to Vera Cruz with this Mexican train, while we took its engine—an ordinary American one—in exchange. We had passed all the fine scenery, and there was nothing of interest save Orizaba, which was still visible for a time. The table-lands are quite barren, save for fields of wheat and rye the first few miles, and after that extensive fields of maguey, or the American aloe, from which "pulque," the national drink, is made. As it was the last of the dry season, the dust was something fearful, and entered the car in clouds, so that, after leaving Esperanza, there was no enjoyment or comfort. "Esperanza" is the Spanish for hope, and we wondered some time why the place was so called, but finally concluded that it must be because after leaving it the traveller's only hope is that he will not be suffocated with dust and tobacco-smoke before he reaches Mexico. The Americans in the car complained of the Spanish custom, and out of pity for the ladies for a while desisted from smoking: but the love of the weed soon overcame them, and the smoke of their pipes and cigars, much stronger than the cigarettes almost universally smoked by the Mexicans, was added to the dust, until from the combination of both it was almost impossible to breathe, and the ladies had to saturate their handkerchiefs with cologne and hold them to their faces to keep from choking. We could not but regret that the latter part of the journey must be disagreeable; but, like Guatemala, Mexico seemed eager to remind us that nowhere on earth could we find perfection, nor in this world be always in regions of beauty; that we were but mortals, and, having been granted a glance at fairyland, we must then come back to the stern realities of human existence and to the trials and woes of mankind.

We found our only entertainment after this at the stations, in watching the strange crowd and in patronizing the venders until we had tasted of all the native productions, one of the principal dishes being "tamales," a sort of turnover filled with a mixture of meat, potato, chili, and dried fruits, and which we found quite palatable, in spite of its peculiar constitution. There, too, was the "pulque," looking like milk and tasting like yeast, made from the aloe or century plant, which grows here in great abundance for miles and miles, and of which we shall speak again later on. The table-lands seemed to be a fine country for stock-raising, and there are numerous haciendas (ranches) and great herds of cattle and sheep, although what they live on in the dry season we could hardly tell, — in fact we could see little but dust. Every ranch has to be surrounded by a great wall, for this is one of the lawless parts of Mexico, the haunt of banditti.

At every station beggars are numerous and very importunate, hideous, ragged, and dirty, the most repulsive looking creatures on the face of the earth. The towns were all very strange in appearance, built of adobe, just the color of the dust in which they stand, and always containing many churches (for the old conquerors were zealous missionaries), and always surrounded by a strong wall for protection against robbers. The names of the places are quite unpronounceable and we troubled ourselves with only one, that of one which impressed us as being the strangest of all strange places we had ever seen; very, very old, with ruined walls and churches, with dust-colored houses, standing in the dust of to-day, with the appearance of being buried in the "dust of ages." A Spanish gentleman (a real Spaniard from Spain), who sat opposite and occasionally conversed with us, gave us the name of the town — Huamantla, a famous robber town, from time immemorial the haunt of robbers and desperadoes. This station is guarded with unusual care, there being, besides the regular guard, three mounted horsemen, powerful looking men, armed with swords and lassos.

Through rows of maguey and through queer old adobe towns, after the sun had set and darkness had closed about us, enveloped in dust and smoke, and listening to tales of blood and adventure in Mexico told by an American behind us, still we sped on for hours over the Mexican plateau to its capital. We arrived about nine o'clock, and once more we felt stranded on a foreign shore, as we felt on arriving at La Tinta, where we spent our first night in the interior of Guatemala. We hardly knew what to do or where to go, until we heard the welcome voice of our Chicago friend and gratefully followed his lead through the rabble of Spanish hackmen to the carriage he had already engaged, and thence to the hotel, where through his kindness we found rooms awaiting us.

Never once in all our journeying did we lack a helping hand. In every time of need some kind friend always appeared to help smooth away our difficulties, and we shall through life retain grateful remembrances of many a one who acted the part of the Good Samaritan.

CHAPTER XVIII.

CITY OF MEXICO.

No country by its nature and history presents greater attractions to the tourist, antiquarian, scientist, student, adventurer, and speculator, than Mexico. It possesses scenery unsurpassed by any in the world; the products of all kingdoms and climes in the greatest abundance; a history most romantic, rich in legend and tradition, in brilliance of exploit, in heroic as well as bloody deeds; a heterogeneous people, of peculiar characteristics and remarkable history, from the Aztec, of unknown origin and pathetic story, to the Spaniard, of marvellous conquest and bloody deeds. Nowhere can there be found grander mountains, fairer valleys, lovelier flowers, a finer climate, more remarkable ruins, or a stranger and more interesting people.

> "Thou Italy of the Occident,
> Land of flowers and summer climes,
> Of holy priests and horrid crimes;
> Land of the cactus and sweet cocoa;

Richer than all the Orient
In gold and glory, in want and woe,
In self-denial, in days misspent,
In truth and treason, in good and guilt,
In ivied ruins and altars low,
In battered walls and blood misspilt,
Glorious, gory Mexico!"

No city in the world, it seems to us, can be, from every point of view, more interesting to visit than the City of Mexico. But let us take the authority of others on this subject. Humboldt, the great naturalist, who has made most extensive investigations there, is most extravagant in his praises. Bayard Taylor, the distinguished traveller, pronounces the City of Mexico, with its surrounding valley, "one of the loveliest scenes of the civilized world." One of England's ministers writes: "Amongst the various capitals of Europe, there are few that can support with any advantage a comparison with Mexico." Steele says it is "a capital that may be as old as Thebes, is as quaint as Tangiers, as foreign as old Spain, and as new as the newest American territory to all modern things"; and Sala, the noted London Journalist: "Of all the strange countries, to me Mexico is the strangest. It is the only country about which I dream; its quaint and picturesque scenery, and tropical products, lingering ever in my imagination."

It is only recently that travel in Mexico has been at all easy; but now that it is fairly opened by railroads, particularly since the building of the Mexican Central, its claim as one of the most interesting places in the world to visit will soon assert itself, and a tide of travel will pour in upon the country. Then, doubtless, more of the conveniences of civilized life will be furnished the tourist; although, if the country loses some of its national characteristics thereby, as is likely, the change will be, in a sense, one to be lamented, for the really appreciative traveller will prefer the grandeur of nature to the comforts of modern life, and the primitive characteristics of Mexico to the elegance of civilized society. The fastidious tourist will find much of which to complain in Mexico, and such a one may go there and perceive little but "dirt, rags, and a strong odor of garlic." These are certainly noticeable, but they must be ignored if one would enjoy Mexico.

'At present there are no really good hotels. The principal one is the Iturbide, once the imperial residence of the first emperor of Mexico after its independence. It is a palatial building of four stories, with five large "patios," and is the fashionable hotel of the city. Adjoining it, and really a part of it, is the San Carlos, of equal respectability. What the traveller especially notices in regard to these, as all Mexican hotels, is the absence of soap and matches (articles never furnished), a scarcity of towels, candles for lighting, single beds, hard pillows, and an abundance of fleas. The plan adopted by many Americans — and one which we pursued — is to take rooms at one of these hotels and then go to a restaurant for meals. The restaurant most highly recommended to us was the Café Anglais, but this from an American standpoint is inferior. Besides the morning cup of coffee there were two meals, breakfast, which was not served until twelve o'clock, and dinner at six. The bill of fare for both meals was almost identical, and soon became monotonous.

The City of Mexico is situated in a beautiful valley, which has an elevation of seven thousand five hundred feet and is completely surrounded by mountains. It is built upon the same spot as the old capital of the Aztecs. But a great physical change has taken place since their time, for their capital was built on an island in Lake Tezcuco, whose waters flowed in canals through every part of the city; while the modern Mexico is built on solid ground. The cause of this change was the diminution of the lake, which is now three miles distant, but which in times of heavy rains threatens to assume its old dominion and flood the city. This danger is further increased by the fact that the level of the lake is only four feet below the great square of Mexico. There have already been several inundations. Once for a period of five years the water stood at such a depth in the streets that boats were used as in the olden times. To obviate this danger various means have been tried, the principal one being the dike of "Nochistongo," the greatest earth-cutting in the world, but as yet unfinished.

The houses of Mexico are of stone, three or four stories high, built in the Spanish style, with patios, balconies, and barred windows. The streets all run at right angles, terminating in a square, but for all that it is difficult for a stranger to find his way, since the exteriors of the houses present one continuous straight wall, so that there are very few landmarks save churches, and, moreover, every block in the street has a separate name and number. Its population is estimated at three hundred thousand. It has almost numberless churches, beautiful gardens and squares, and fine avenues.

The climate is justly celebrated, though to us not so agreeable as that of Guatemala, of somewhat less elevation. The region is one of perpetual summer, with flowers and fruits the year round. The temperature ranges from sixty-five to eighty-five degrees; it is quite warm in the middle of the day, but always cool morning and night. The rarefied air is said to affect the breathing, though we noticed no unpleasant sensation, except a restlessness and sleeplessness, which may have been due to the exhilarating effects of the atmosphere, and which made it impossible for us to take a siesta. The city itself is not as healthy as some others in Mexico, for example Puebla. This is due to the fact of a lack of drainage, which causes malaria and typhus fever, and would, if not for the great elevation, make the city very unhealthy. Pneumonia is quite prevalent, and "taking cold" is greatly dreaded.

Before describing the city let us look back a

little into its past, that we may the better understand the people and the scenes we witness.

When Cortez and his army, in 1520, after their perilous and adventurous march from the coast, came to the present site of Mexico, they found the capital of a kingdom which astonished them for its wealth, power, and magnificence, — the kingdom of the Aztecs, who came into Mexico at the close of the thirteenth century. Who these Aztecs were, or whence they came, is still a mystery. Some have tried to identify them with the lost tribes of Israel, others believe they are of Asiatic origin; but whoever they were, it is certain they were a wonderful people, for the Spaniards, from the most advanced country of Europe at that time, were astonished at their civilization. Prescott gives us the Spaniards' first impression of the capital as follows: "Like some Indian Empress with her coronal of pearls — the fair city of Mexico, with her white towers and pyramidal temples, reposing as it were on the bosom of the waters, — the far famed 'Venice of the Aztecs.'"

At the entrance of the city the Spaniards were met by the royal retinue, which advanced with as much pomp as that of an Oriental prince: "Amidst a crowd of Indian nobles, preceded by three officers of state, bearing golden wands, they saw the royal palanquin blazing with burnished gold. It was borne on the shoulders of nobles, and over it a canopy of gaudy feather work, powdered with jewels and fringed with silver, was supported by four attendants of the same rank. When the train had come within a convenient distance, Montezuma descended from his litter, leaning on the arms of two lords, and the obsequious attendants strewed the ground with cotton tapestry that his imperial feet might not be contaminated by the rude soil. His subjects, who lined the sides of the causeway, bent forward with their eyes fastened on the ground as he passed, and some of the humbler classes prostrated themselves before him."

"Montezuma wore the girdle and ample square cloak, 'tilmatli,' of his nation. It was made of the finest cotton, with the embroidered ends gathered in a knot round his neck. His feet were defended by sandals having soles of gold, and the leathern thongs which bound them to his ankles were embossed with the same metal. Both the cloak and sandals were sprinkled with pearls and precious stones. On his head he wore no other ornament than a 'panache' of plumes of the royal green, which floated down his back, the badge of military rank."

When they entered the city they were still further filled with admiration and wonder. The excellence of the architecture astonished them, and they pronounced the best of the buildings equal to those in Spain. The houses were of stone from the quarries, with flat roofs covered with gardens, and with walls of scented wood, hung with rich tapestries and feather work. The buildings covered large spaces of ground, that of Montezuma being described as so extensive that the whole could not be traversed at one time without the greatest fatigue. There were beautiful gardens, a large aviary, menageries of wild beasts, and an immense market place in which were gathered products and riches from the whole realm. The emperor presented them with rich gifts of gold, silver, emeralds, pearls, and other precious stones, which dazzled the eyes of the avaricious Spaniards and made them long for conquest.

The people, too, were quite advanced in the mechanical arts, agriculture, and weaving; their fabrics were of great fineness and beauty; their feather work, of which some remnant remains at the present day, was remarkable; and the work of their silversmiths the Spaniards pronounced superior to their own. Even allowing much for exaggeration on the part of the Spaniards, there is no doubt but this was a remarkable kingdom and one seeing the Indians of to-day in Mexico can hardly realize that they can be the direct descendants of the gifted Aztecs, until he remembers what the long years of oppression under the Spanish rule must have done, and the fact that in spite of all this the best beloved President of Mexico, Juarez, was a full-blooded Indian.

In the conquest of Mexico the noblest of the Aztecs fell, and the Spaniards married the highborn Indian maidens, so that while about four-fifths of the population are Indians, the remainder are "mestizos," with the exception of some Castilians and foreigners.

Our first impressions of the people we have already given as very unfavorable, because of the desperate-looking men we saw, the great necessity for military force to insure safety in travelling, and the deeds of blood and cruelty which are even now committed. But in the City of Mexico we saw pleasanter faces, and many tourists are very favorably impressed by the people. They are very courteous and polite, as are all Spanish people, every man, however poor, being a gentleman. But we were much less pleased with them than the Guatemaltecans, with whom we naturally compared them. They seemed to us less honest, more cruel, and less intelligent; at any rate, not nearly as quick in understanding poor Spanish, for to a Guatemaltecan we need say only a few words and all our wants would be understood, if they had not already been anticipated, but to a Mexican we must give a full and correct sentence before we could get anything, and were often out of patience with his stupidity.

We wondered much why there should be such a difference between the people of these two adjoining countries, both having been originally occupied by Indians, conquered and settled by Spaniards, and under Spanish rule for about the same length of time. It seemed to us that part of the answer lay in the difference in the Indian blood, the Indians of Guatemala being descended from the Toltecs, who are supposed to have been superior to the

Aztecs, as less warlike, more gentle and industrious, and, above all, not cannibals or practisers of the terrible rite of human sacrifice, which stained the history of the Aztecs. We noticed at once a difference between the Mexican and Guatemala Indians. Though of the same general appearance and charcteristics, the Mexican Indians are rather larger, less cleanly and less honest, and with less attractive faces. But this will not account for all the difference, and, doubtless, more is due to the fact that Mexico's great natural resources and the stories of its fabulous wealth have attracted to it many of the worst and most adventurous of all nations.

With no thought of business, our whole time now was given to sight-seeing, in company with the two friends from Chicago, who greatly enhanced our pleasure and profit, for, having travelled so long alone, we were pleased to find companions who not only were most agreeable, but were also accustomed to travelling, and understood well the art of sight-seeing.

The street scenes in the City of Mexico were more fascinating to us than any panorama or museum, and it was a perfect delight, an experience ever new and ever fresh, simply to walk the streets and view the people, — this "quaint, primitive, slow, and picturesque people." There are the Indians, the direct descendants of the old Aztecs, who once held sway in this fertile valley. To-day they still dwell here, the same race whom Cortez conquered, changed and still unchanged. They have transferred their worship of idols to that of the Virgin; their feasts and holy days in honor of their gods to the saints of the Catholic Church. They have learned the Spanish language (some of them), but that is about all. They still dress in much the same fashion, eat the same food, build their houses as of old, raise vegetables and flowers, sell goods in the market place, and make rag figures and the beautiful feather work which so enchanted Cortez. Whole villages exactly as they were three hundred years ago, aqueducts all bringing water into the City of Mexico, and the famous "floating gardens," still exist as their monuments. We meet these Indians at every turn, and forget their dirt and rags in the thought of their wonderful history. Nowhere else is there to be found a more primitive people — a people so long remaining unchanged, a people conquered but not subdued, brought low but not enslaved, ruled over but still ruling.

Besides these we met the "caballero," in European dress; the "fair señorita" of pure Castilian blood, dressed in the conventional black and wearing the graceful Spanish mantilla; the "charro," or Mexican rider, in his striking costume, on a horse with magnificent trappings; troops of soldiers in uniform; venders of lottery tickets as thick as flies; the loathsome "lepéros," and the quaint and pleasant-faced "aguador," or water-carrier — these two latter in striking contrast, one the most repulsive, the other the most interesting personage of the streets of Mexico. The former is a ragged and dirty "mestizo," one of the vilest specimens of humanity, a born thief and murderer. He meets you at every turn, being especially prominent in the cathedrals on feast days; importunes you for money in a whining, monotonous tone "por Dios"; is ever on the lookout to steal your watch and money; and, if any one wants to be rid of you, "will kill you for a dollar." There is no place where greater care must be exercised against pickpockets. It has almost passed into a proverb that every American who comes to Mexico loses his watch, but we met with no trouble whatever of this kind.

The "aguador," whom we always liked to meet, is as honest as the "lepéro" is dishonest, and shows it in his kindly face. His business is to convey water from the various fountains throughout the city to the houses. His dress is a queer suit of leather, and on his back, from a leather strap, hangs a large earthen jar, while in his hands he carries a water pitcher. Always with the same kind, unvarying expression and statuesque pose, he looks like some queer figure that has suddenly stepped out of an old museum and taken on the power of locomotion.

The trade of "cargador," or burden-bearing, is followed as extensively in Mexico as in Guatemala. Almost everything used in the great city is borne on the backs of men. It was no uncommon sight to see a piano being carried by three or four men, for there is no other express. A company was started a while ago by a New York firm, but it proved a failure.

CHAPTER XIX.

IN AND ABOUT THE PLAZA.

As in the old Roman Empire "all roads lead to Rome," so in Mexico all streets lead to the Plaza Mayor, and every morning, after taking our coffee, we wended our way thither, and then started on the excursion we had planned for the day. The Plaza is the great central square of the city, from which lines of horse-cars run in all directions. On its four sides are the great cathedral, the National Palace, and the "portales," or open arcades, where there are numberless shops lining both sides of the pavement. In the centre of the square is the pleasure garden called the "zocalo," with beautiful flowers and trees, among which are found both the palm and the pine growing together, a sight seen in but few parts of the world. There is music here two or three times a week, and then the scene is a gay one, for the garden is thronged with all classes, from the highest to the lowest. Venders of curious Mexican products are of course numerous, among whom are small boys calling "nieve" (Mexican ice-cream), which tastes, as its name would indicate, like half melted snow with a little vanilla flavoring. Real ice-cream is not known here, although it would be refreshing in this climate; but ice is a luxury and has to be manufactured by machinery or brought down from Popocatapetl on mules' backs. Formerly all the ice used by the city was supplied from the icicles of this volcano.

Instead of ice-cream there are fruit-drinks of various kinds, which are most refreshing, although rather too sweet for the American taste. All along on one side of the "zocalo" is a row of white, gayly decorated tents, where these drinks are sold. The principal are "limonada" (from the lime), "tamarinda" (from the tamarind), "chia" (from a fruit unknown to us), "orchata" (from melon seeds), and "piña" (from the pineapple). We never passed these tents without patronizing one of them, which was on an average about twice a day, and we had many and long struggles to get the "limonada" sour enough to suit one of the party.

The "pulque," which is the national drink, is not sold in such an attractive manner, but is carted about in skins of black pigs. As has been before stated, the "pulque" is made from the maguey or century-plant, as we call it, which, on the plains of Mexico, attains a great size, its leaves being sometimes ten feet long. The sap of the plant is extracted by an Indian, who draws it out through a gourd by suction. A single plant yields from two to seven quarts a day, and is valued at ten dollars. The sap when first removed is sweet, and appropriately called "aguamiel," or honey-water. This allowed to ferment about twenty-four hours becomes "pulque," which contains about six per cent of alcohol. It looks very much like buttermilk, and has a sour, disagreeable odor and taste (to any but a Mexican), but is said to be a refreshing drink and a most excellent promoter of digestion, and Europeans and Americans can learn to like it. Further fermented it becomes "mescal," which is very intoxicating, containing about as much alcohol as whiskey. "Pulque" was invented by the Toltecs, who were as fond of it as the Mexicans are to-day, and some idea of the estimation in which it is now held may be gained from the fact that a daily train is run from the "maguey" district, one hundred miles from Mexico, to the city, for the sole transportation of "pulque," from which the railroad derives a revenue of one thousand dollars a day. The plant is also put to many other uses, the leaves being used for thatching and for making paper, the fibres for making thread and twine, the thorns for needles.

The great cathedral at the head of the Plaza is the most prominent building in all Mexico, and is said to be the largest church on the American continent. It is built on the very spot of the old Aztec temple, which was destroyed by Cortez in 1530. The cost was two million dollars, notwithstanding the fact that most of the labor was free, the Indians working from a spirit of devotion.

The exterior is very beautiful, with elaborate stucco work, and the interior still rich, although it has been stripped of its greatest wealth by the successive plunderings which have occurred in various times of revolution and invasion. Leading from the main body of the house are twenty-five chapels, each with its own altar and saint. So vast is this great church that forty priests can say mass at the same time without interference, and a company of ten thousand soldiers make scarcely any impression.

When the clerical party was at the height of its power and possessed nearly all the wealth of Mexico, the great altar in the centre of the cathedral was the richest in the world, and it is now magnificent, although it has lost many rich treasures, such as gold crosses, censers and chalices studded with precious gems, golden candlesticks heavier than a man could lift, and statues of gold set with diamonds. The church is still adorned with exceedingly beautiful frescoes and paintings by celebrated artists, but the general effect of the interior is rather of gorgeousness than elegance.

We happened to be in Mexico during Lent, when almost every day is a feast day, when the churches are all draped, all the ladies go to mass in black, and services are frequently and faithfully attended. The cathedral seemed to be crowded all the time with rich and poor, high and low alike; the beautiful señora could be seen kneeling on the stone floor beside a ragged Indian with a load on his back, and the proud Spaniard close beside the dirty beggar. Palm Sunday the cathedral was so crowded that we could scarcely find standing room, and the air so close and odorous that we were thankful to get out as soon as possible. There was a gay scene before the church, where hundreds of Indian women were sitting, weaving the palm leaves into various pretty and curious shapes, and decorating them with bright-colored poppies. Everybody carried one of these palms, and the bright color of the poppies setting off the yellow background of the leaf made the streets look bright and gay.

Almost every day of this week was a feast day to some saint or saints, and had its own particular observances. One of the most curious superstitions is shown in the fact that all the children as they go about the streets Thursday swing a rattle with great vehemence, and firmly believe that the noise will "drive the devil out of town." Sometimes these rattles are attached to a grotesque image of the arch-fiend, but in whatever form they are made, they are swung by the small boys with great delight, and fill the air with noise enough to banish Satan and all his host. On Good Friday the people take it upon themselves to execute vengeance upon Judas. Numberless effigies of the betrayer, filled with explosives, are paraded about the streets and blown up by the boys amidst great enthusiasm. Saturday morning immense figures of Judas are stretched across the streets, very many being hung in front of the cathedral, and at 10 A. M. all the bells ring with great clamor, the drapings fall in the churches, fire-works are set off, and the images of Judas are exploded in the midst of great rejoicing. Easter Sunday is of course the great festal day; then the churches are beautifully decorated, and the people leave off their black and appear in gay holiday attire.

These observances still exist, although the power of the church has been broken. Priests and nuns are forbidden to appear in the streets in their characteristic dress, on penalty of imprisonment, but the people still show them great adoration. We one day saw the people all kneeling as a bishop descended from his carriage, and often saw young men kiss the hand of a priest with greatest adulation. Formerly there were frequent religious processions, in which some image was carried through the streets, and everybody was required to remain kneeling while it passed, but this kept the people on their knees the greater portion of the time, and interfered so seriously with business that the processions were finally abolished.

As it was Lent there were few amusements in the city, the theatres all being closed, but on Palm Sunday at one of them the Passion Play was given, and after some debate we decided to go. It seemed to us that the natural environment of the play there, the character and religion of the people, and the spirit with which it would be given and witnessed would make it an entirely different affair from the same play anywhere else in the world save in Oberammergau itself, where it is purely a matter of religion, a holy and sacred rite on the part of all the participants. In this opinion we were not disappointed, and were very glad we witnessed the play, for it was most impressive throughout — a wonderful commentary on the Bible narrative.

The play began at four o'clock in the afternoon and lasted until after nine o'clock. It was in seven acts, and the waits between were quite long; still it was not wearisome. Each scene had a solemnity about it that kept the audience under a spell so that the intervals were not noticed, the mind being fully occupied with what had been presented.

The whole effect of the play was very similar to that produced by looking at pictures upon the same subject, although far more impressive. The costumes, attitudes and scenes were copied with the greatest faithfulness from the paintings of the great artists. For instance, "The Last Supper" was a living embodiment of the well-known picture of Da Vinci, faithful to the smallest detail. In all the scenes it was remarkable how closely the faces of all the actors resembled those made familiar to everybody by these paintings, and there is no doubt but that these people, belonging, as we have reason to believe, to an Oriental race, are by natural endowment and cast of features better adapted than almost any other, certainly better than the German race, to enact this play.

The dialogue was, of course, all in Spanish, a beautiful and quite faithful rendering of the Bible account, and the fact that we could not understand the whole perfectly only served to heighten the effect, enough being understood to keep the mind fully acquainted with the progress of the action, and not enough to detract from the high conception of the scene. In some instances there were no words spoken, particularly in the scene of the crucifixion — the most powerful of all, a scene wonderfully realistic and most impressive.

In the whole play from beginning to end there was nothing that could be discordant or disagreeable to the most religious person. Quite the contrary: the whole seemed more weighty and powerful than any sermon could be on the same subject. Still it does not in the least follow that its production in this country should be encouraged or supported; for, although most fitting and effectual among the simple people, who attended with reverence and religious feelings, it would be an entirely different thing in this country and among our mixed population. In Mexico the play was in its proper setting, but here it would not be. There it was a religious act, here it would be sacrilege.

Since 1862 there have been Protestant missions in Mexico, and they now number fifteen. The work was at first very slow and discouraging, and met with great opposition, even so much that the lives of Protestants were in great danger, but the missions are now quite well established. In the City of Mexico there are ten Protestant congregations, three of which hold services every Sunday in English.

Many curious remains have been unearthed in the spot where the cathedral now stands, and where the Aztec temple once stood. Among them is the famous "calendar stone" of the Aztecs, supposed to have been used in computing time, although this is not certain. It is a large stone, weighing twenty-six tons, hewn out of basalt from distant quarries, and completely covered with sculpture, attesting to the skill of the Aztecs. It is now inserted in the side of the present cathedral. In the "zocalo" is a rockery composed of lava from the volcano and of idols dug out of this spot — idols of various forms and sizes, making a curious collection.

Prescott describes a visit which Cortez made to the old heathen temple at Montezuma's invitation. The temple or "teocalli," as it was called, is described as pyramidal, built of stone, and with five stories, decreasing in size. The ascent was made by a flight of steps on the outside and was so tiresome that Montezuma provided priests to carry himself and Cortez, but the latter refused the offer, preferring to march at the head of his men, saying, "The Spaniards are never weary." On the summit they found a vast area paved with stones, and had a magnificent view of the city and surroundings, so magnificent that Cortez could not restrain his excessive admiration.

Montezuma showed them the gods of the Aztecs and the implements used in their worship. There was the sacrificial stone of jasper, nine feet high and twenty-seven feet in circumference. On this stone, it is said, upwards of sixty thousand victims were sacrificed, the heart being cut out of the living victim by the priest and offered to the god of war. Many of the brave Spaniards met this fate, for all who could be taken alive were thus sacrificed. They were shown also the circular drum, of serpents' skins, whose melancholy sound was the signal to arouse the whole city to arms, and which not long afterward, when the siege of Mexico had begun, smote on the ears of the Spaniards like a death knell. Then they were taken into the sanctuaries of the gods, the principal one being "Huitzilopotxtli," god of war, a colossal, hideous image, his chief ornament being a chain of gold and silver hearts about his neck, while on the altar before him lay three human hearts just torn from their victims. They saw other altars and sanctuaries, and were horrified at the sight of this pagan worship. They declared "the stench was more intolerable than that of the slaughter-houses in Castile, and the frantic forms of priests, with their dark robes clotted with blood, as they flitted to and fro, seemed to be the very ministers of Satan."

The entire east side of the Plaza is occupied by the National Palace or government building, capable, it is said, of lodging ten thousand persons. It is open to visitors on application to the Governor. The troops are reviewed every morning in front of this building, and an appearance of power and authority is always maintained by guards at frequent intervals. There was quite a military display in the city while we were there, as it was the time of the troubles in Guatemala, to which troops were being sent, and companies of soldiers frequently paraded the streets with bands of music.

When we had the courage to run the gauntlet of haggling peddlers we used to walk the length of the "portales" and gaze with wonder and curiosity on the various little shops standing as thick as possible on both sides. In our large cities we have many stands and petty merchants, but nothing to compare with Mexico. There, if a man possesses one article, he will set himself up for a merchant. A fellow importuned us one day to buy of him a canary bird which he held in his hand. Often a gilt mirror or a cheap picture would bear the sign "se vende" (for sale), and this one article would constitute the man's sole stock in trade. Some of the stands, in fact, most of them, have a variety of goods, not even surpassed by the "Old Curiosity Shop." For instance, there would be candy, old iron, fruit, lace, spurs and bits, ribbon, beads, Aztec idols, knives and forks, crosses, amulets, and dolls, all in one confused array at the same little stand. Just as in Guatemala, you must always haggle with the merchant and give him less than half his first price. But the peddlers who go about the streets are the most annoying, and it is quite as hard to get rid of them as of a beggar, — "No," and "I do not want it," making no impression whatever, unless it be to redouble their efforts. We must give one or two examples of the experiences of this kind that we had to undergo many times a day.

A boy meets us with tortoise-shell combs and asks us to buy. They are really a very nice article, and we inquire the price.

"Diez y seis reales" ($2.00), the boy answers.

"No; that is too much."

"Doce reales" ($1.50).

"Too much. I don't want it."

More earnestly, "Ocho reales" ($1.00).

"No; I don't want it," and we turn to go away.

Then he eagerly asks, "How much will you give?"

"Cuatro reales" (50 cents).

Whereupon, to our own surprise, the boy immediately closes the bargain, and we have his two dollar comb for fifty cents.

Another time we are met by a man with canes to sell.

We shake our heads and say, "No, no," as emphatically as possible, and walk on; but he follows us, trying to get us to look at his canes, and giving us the prices, five and six dollars. We say that is very dear ("muy caro"). He comes down dollar after dollar, and we keep saying "No," and that we do not want his canes, but he pays not the slightest attention and seems the more determined to sell us one because we declare we do not want it. Then comes the invariable question, "How much will you give?" We answer emphatically that "We do not want *any* canes at *any* price"; but that does not in the least discourage him. Finally, after he has followed us the whole length of the street and repeated the same questions over and over, we decide to make him an offer that will silence him, and, in sheer desperation, say we will give a "medio." At that he turns on his heel and walks off with such a look of injured innocence, disgust, and astonishment that we almost repent our own escape. That a sane person could be capable of such audacity as to offer five cents for a five-dollar article is evidently more than he had ever imagined possible even for an American.

This method, although not entirely satisfactory to ourselves, was the only one we ever found that was at all effectual. When all other experiments failed we turned to this as a final resort, and would commend it to all travellers in Mexico who have the courage to bear the sad effect produced on the zealous peddler.

CHAPTER XX.

RAMBLES ABOUT THE CITY.

NEAR the Plaza is situated the market, which, as we have before stated, is always an interesting place to visit in these countries. This market was more crowded than any we had ever seen; in fact, it was almost impossible to make one's way about among the people and the wares which thickly covered the ground.

But most interesting of all to us were the bright, black-eyed boys, of ten or twelve, whose business it is to carry purchases in the baskets which they bear on their heads. As soon as our party of four entered, we were at once besought by six or seven of these little fellows who looked upon us as desirable patrons, — for Americans have a great reputation among them for being rich, and it is as easy in Mexico to recognize an American as for us to recognize a Chinaman in our streets. We observed this fact with interest, and could not only distinguish a party of Americans as soon as we saw them, but could almost tell by their appearance just how long they had been in Mexico, and to what place of interest they were then going.

But to return to the boys. Never in their lives have they known what play is. As soon as they could walk, they began to work; but still, the fun and mischief inherent in the boy nature was there, and, with bright faces and laughing eyes, they eagerly looked up at us, and all talking together as fast as possible, entreated us to hire them. We declared we did not need their services, but they only redoubled their efforts, and talked away in such a lively, good-natured manner that we smiled, too, in spite of our attempts to look severe. My father got impatient over the delay — for not understanding a word he failed to see the fun — and said, "Why don't you send them away? If I could speak Spanish I would get rid of those boys." How many times a day every impatient American in Mexico makes this remark! If he "could speak Spanish," he thinks he could reform the country; could turn slow-going Mexico into enterprising Boston; make the waiters jump to do his bidding, and the servants bound at his call. But he might just as well think of making a snail go at a hare's pace. Mexico is slow and the Mexicans are slow, and will be in spite of all that Americans speaking Spanish, English, or any other language can do to make them otherwise; and as nothing except their ill-will can be gained by impatience and anger, you might just as well when you are there resign yourself to their easy, careless ways, give up New England push and hurry, and in this way only really enjoy Mexico.

But that remark, "If I could speak Spanish," roused two of us, who really pretended we could, to vindicate ourselves and redeem our reputation; so we summoned all our knowledge and dignity and bade the boys go away, but they only laughed the more and talked the faster, in such a merry way that we laughed too, and let them follow us about as long as they wished. One among them never deserted us, never failed to see us as soon as we entered, and lingered after the others had gone, even until we left the market. He had a bright, pleasant face that we shall always remember, and we are perfectly confident that, with the advantages of education and training, he would be a superior man. Those of the Mexicans who have come north to be educated have shown marked ability. We know of two in particular, who came not understanding a word of English, and soon surpassed all others in the school they attended, winning the highest prizes for scholarship. But this boy who so interested us, will never have the advantages of an education, and it is truly sad to think of him, and multitudes of others, without any chance in life to improve and develop their God-given powers.

In the most beautiful faces of men and women, — and nowhere can there be seen more beautiful faces, — we remarked this lack, which made their beauty simply physical, wanting in the truest requisites. The children, however, before they have lost their youthful innocence and grace, are truly beautiful, but time brings to them no added wisdom or spirituality.

We once saw a child, a girl of five or six years, who certainly had the loveliest face we had ever seen — a face lovely enough for one of Raphael's angels. With her was her mother, who, as we saw from the regularity of her features, was once just as fair, but, though still young, she had lost the grace of childhood and gained nothing in intelligence, or strength of character. From a beautiful child she had become, as her looks indicated, an ordinary vapid woman, and such would the child before us become in her turn. The Mexican women, like the women of other Spanish countries, are noted for their beauty, but it is of short duration, for they begin to fade as soon as married, which is very young, and are old at thirty. The majority of them, too, judging from those we saw, use so much paint and powder that they completely conceal what natural beauty they do have. The universality of this foolish practice, and the extent to which it is carried, has no parallel in any country in which we have ever been. It seemed to us, comparing the two countries, that Guatemala was noticeable for its handsome women, Mexico for its magnificent looking men.

One day while in the city we spent in shopping, particularly for curiosities, for there are several articles of Mexican production as yet but little known. Among them is the feather-work already mentioned. The Indians, with the real feathers, fashion on a card a perfect representation of birds of every kind known to them. The skill shown in making these beautiful objects is remarkable, and the process is a secret unknown save to a few, who guard it jealously as a sacred legacy from their Aztec ancestors. Another relic of the old days is the "rag figures," most life-like representations of every class of society, and considered by many to surpass the best work of the Chinese or Japanese. There is also to tempt the tourist the filagree silver-work, in which the Mexicans excel; the opals of greatest variety; the beautiful onyx, which is polished and shaped into various forms; and numerous little idols, supposed to have been made by the old Aztecs, but in many cases imitations but a few days old.

One of the most interesting places in the city to visit is the "Grand National Museum." The court of this building is very beautiful, with flowers and trees, and in the midst of it is the great sacrificial stone, already mentioned as used by the Aztecs in their pagan worship. It is an immense stone, weighing many tons, and completely covered with curious carving, which must have required great skill and labor. In the centre is a hollow well, from which a canal runs to the edge of the stone, evidently for the purpose of conveying away the blood of the victim. Standing behind this stone is the old image of the war-god, to whom these sacrifices were made, — a huge, hideous, shapeless figure, cut out of solid rock.

In a room off this court we saw the gilded coach of Maximilian. While we were looking at it some Indians from the country were gazing at it with wonder and admiration. They had come into the city to celebrate some feast day, and strangely enough, as it seemed to us, were visiting the museum. Ascending the stairs, we found quite an extensive museum, containing a most interesting and valuable collection. Besides the mineral, animal, and vegetable products of the country are many curiosities; portraits of the old Spanish viceroys, among them that of Cortez; the banner and other relics of the great conqueror, and the suit of armor worn by his lieutenant Alvarado; the rich silver plate of Maximilian; Aztec idols; pottery, pictures of ruins, and much that is valuable and interesting to the archæologist for its antiquity and the skill it shows the Aztecs to have possessed. The Indians we have mentioned seemed to regard us with quite as much interest as anything in the museum, and showed a great desire to talk with us. They followed us about, calling our attention to whatever was to them especially noticeable, and the amount of understanding and appreciation that they showed in all they saw was quite surprising.

Another notable institution is the Academy of San Carlos, built in the reign of Charles III. of Spain. It contains fine specimens of paintings, statuary, and steel engravings. There are works of Leonardo da Vinci, Murillo, Van Dycke, and Canova, besides fine paintings by old and modern Mexican artists, among whom is Velasco, who has taken the beautiful valley of Mexico for his subject, and has produced some very fine landscapes. While we were being shown about, an old gentleman came and talked with us, one who evidently had a love and appreciation for pictures, and great pride in the place. The academy seemed to be a school for artists, and we were really surprised at the interest and advancement this nation had evidently made in art.

Another building attesting to the advancement of Mexico and interest in education is the School of Mines, for the purpose of giving a particular knowledge on the subject of mining. The building, called one of the finest in Mexico, cost two million dollars, and is the one in which Grant was entertained. It has a fine and extensive collection of rocks, minerals, and fossils, belonging to Mexico; but a lack of system in the arrangement of the specimens was most noticeable. The Mexicans do not seem to pay as much attention to classification as we do.

One place in which we were disappointed was the National Pawn-Shop, situated opposite the cathedral, and one of the oldest houses in the city, once the residence of Cortez. The guide-book says: "Pearls, rubies, emeralds, and diamonds in great numbers dazzle the visitor's sight," and we went several times to see the rich treasures supposed to be stored there, but without seeing anything of special interest. We made inquiries each time of the uniformed official at the door if there was not more to see, and he invariably told us to come "mañana." Indeed, in our sight-seeing this word was continually bringing us to a standstill and defeating our plans. It is a word that the traveller in Mexico soon learns; for he hears it continually. We had the following experience near the close of our stay, when we felt that time was precious. We visited the pawn-shop first in search of some souvenir or curios, but, as usual, were told to come "mañana." Then we went to the academy of San Carlos, where, having a permit from the palace, we were admitted, but strongly advised by the old gentleman in attendance to come "mañana," because then the artists would be at liberty, and would be pleased to talk with us about the pictures. To prevent ourselves from being sent away, we had to protest that we should leave Mexico "to-morrow," and should not have another opportunity to come. Going next to the "Money Exchange," we found it closed, as well as many of the principal stores, and, inquiring of an American, elicited the expected answer that they were closed because it was a feast day, and would not be open until *to-morrow*. We next proceeded to one of the bathing establishments, for which Mexico is noted, supposing of course that they would be open always, but at one after another all the satisfaction we could get was "mañana," "mañana," and we were obliged to go to five before we could gain admittance. That night, on returning to the hotel, we inquired for our laundry, which should have been there the day before, and the smiling clerk assured us in the most hopeful tone that the washwoman would come "mañana sin falta" (to-morrow without fail), but when we saw that laundry again we had been home fully one week. It was not brought back to the hotel until after our departure, and travelled all the way from Mexico a few days behind us, a silent but able witness of the procrastinating and dilatory character of Mexico and of "mañana," the halcyon Spanish time — the time that never comes but is always coming, the time that never was but will always be. "Mañana" the Mexican will see you on business; "mañana" your Spanish friend will keep his appointment; "mañana" the servants will execute your commands; *to-morrow* you can have *everything* you wish, but *to-day nothing*. "No time like the present" is transformed by the Spanish into, "no time like to-morrow." They work, plan, execute "mañana," but rest, eat, sleep, and take their ease to-day. More true of them even than of us are the words of Shakespeare : —

> To-morrow and to-morrow and to-morrow
> Creeps on its petty pace from day to day,
> To the last syllable of recorded time;
> And all our yesterdays have lighted fools
> The way to dusty death.

CHAPTER XXI.

EXCURSIONS IN THE SUBURBS.

By taking a trip in any line of horse-cars starting from the Plaza, a very delightful excursion can be made, in the midst always of beautiful scenery and curious sights. Of these excursions we will mention but few.

One day we went to the "Shrine of Guadalupe," about three miles distant from the city, the most sacred place of worship in the country; so sacred that some devotees crawl all the way from the City of Mexico on their hands and knees to visit it. On a steep hill stands the chapel dedicated to the Virgin Mary, who is believed to have appeared on this spot to a poor Indian shepherd, and commanded him to go to the bishop and tell her wish that a church be built. The bishop was skeptical until the Virgin had appeared several times, caused flowers to spring up miraculously, and finally stamped her image on the

Indian's blanket. Then he was convinced, and a chapel was built on the hill and a magnificent church, costing eight hundred thousand dollars, on the plain below, one of the objects of interest in the church being an altar-rail of pure silver, worth several thousand dollars.

It was a long climb, by winding stone steps, to the top of the hill, but we were rewarded with a fine view. In front of the chapel is a strange monument in the form of a mast and sails carved from stone, the gift of a sailor who escaped shipwreck at sea; and in the chapel are numerous offerings testifying to miraculous cures; even the blanket is there, with the image stamped upon it, to convince all disbelievers. Behind the church is a burying-ground, and fabulous sums are paid to be buried here. Among other graves is that of Santa Anna.

Another day, starting off in a different direction, we had a delightful ride through several of the suburban towns, and visited the historic tree of "la noche triste," — the tree under which Cortez is said to have encamped after the disaster to his army on that sad night when he was obliged to flee from the City of Mexico with such terrible loss. The tree is one of the cypresses which in Mexico attain such enormous size, has a knotted gnarled trunk of huge proportions, and gives abundant proof of its age. It is now surrounded by an iron fence, on account of attempts of the Indians to destroy it in order to show their hatred of the Spaniards. The events of the "sad night" are described by Prescott in the most graphic manner.

On the death of Montezuma, the only tie between the Spaniards and the natives was broken, and the Spaniards were obliged to evacuate the city. They chose a dark night, when all was wrapt in silence, and began their march as noiselessly as possible; but as they reached the canal and were laying their portable bridge, which would bring them in comparative safety on the other shore, "several Indian sentinels, who had been stationed there, took the alarm and fled, rousing their countrymen by their cries. The priests, keeping night watch on the summit of the 'teocallis,' instantly caught the tidings and sounded their shells, while the huge drum of serpent skins, in the desolate temple of the war-god, sent forth those solemn notes which, heard only in seasons of calamity, vibrated through every corner of the capital. The Spaniards saw there was no time to be lost. But before they could cross, a gathering sound was heard like that of a mighty forest agitated by the winds. It grew louder and louder, while on the dark waters of the lake was heard a splashing noise as of many oars. Then came stones and arrows falling every moment faster and more furious, till they thickened into a terrible tempest, while the very heavens were rent with yells and war cries of myriads of combatants who seemed all at once to be swarming over land and lake."

"The carnage raged fearfully all along the length of the causeway." Confusion and disorder reigned supreme, and the voice of Cortez was lost in the great uproar. Many of the cavaliers plunged into the water, and some succeeded in swimming across, but many were cut down by the Aztecs, or dragged on board their canoes to meet a worse death on the sacrificial stone; or, reaching the bank, were rolled headlong down the steep. At the third breach Alvarado is said to have performed his wonderful feat of "clearing the wide gap at a leap," so remarkable an achievement that the Indians gave him the name "Tonatiuh" (the child of the sun). The spot where this occurred is now a street called "El Salto de Alvarado" (Alvarado's leap), and the conductor pointed it out to us as we passed it.

Cortez and a portion of his army escaped, and reached the village of Popotla, where they halted. It is said that Cortez, although accustomed to conceal his feelings, covered his face with his hands, and wept as he looked in vain for some of his bravest cavaliers, and beheld the disabled and disordered company — all that was left of his once proud and powerful army. That after this he could ever return and conquer this great empire seemed almost incredible, and ranks with the great exploits of romance.

At the southeast end of the city there is a remnant of the "fair Venice of the Aztecs" in the Viga canal, with its floating gardens leading to the lakes Chalco and Xochimilco. At the place where the canal enters the city the scene, especially in the morning, is a busy and interesting one, the water being covered with flat-bottomed boats poled by Indians and loaded with vegetables and flowers. Very often there is a flower-show here, and the Indians, who have retained the old Aztec characteristic of love of flowers, expose for sale most beautiful bouquets, as artistic as those of our best florists; large bouquets of roses, which here would sell for five or six dollars, being sold there for twenty-five or thirty-seven and a half cents. Along the canal is a fine avenue lined on both sides with large trees, and at these flower-shows this avenue is filled with coaches and horsemen, composing the *élite* of the town. There are many fanciful booths trimmed with palm leaves and poppies; two bands of music play alternately, and the street is thronged with a gay company. The whole scene betokens a holiday festivity, and one such occasion with us would be considered gayety enough for a period of years, but the Mexicans repeat them almost every week, such a land is theirs for mirth and music, for flowers and fruit, for joy and sunshine!

There are numerous boats, with awnings and cushioned seats, to be engaged at fifty cents or one dollar an hour, for an excursion up the canal. These are poled by Indians, and remind one somewhat of the gondolas of Venice. We selected one from the numerous boatmen who eagerly sought our patronage, and were soon gently gliding over the smooth water. It was a perfect day, as were all our days in Mexico; the sky was bright, cloudless, and beautifully blue, and the whole atmosphere was pervaded by such peace and quiet as must have reigned in the Garden of Eden. The most careless and unappreciative person could not fail to come under the spell, and banish for the time all thought of the world and its strife.

As we glided on we passed fine avenues of trees and queer old adobe villages, unchanged in the lapse of time. We ourselves were the only feature of the scene that did not belong to ages past; for in the reign of Montezuma these same towns stood here, the same willows grew on the banks, and just such boats, loaded with vegetables and flowers, and poled by Indians with precisely the same appearance, passed up and down this canal. Where else in the world can be found a more interesting primitive scene? And, although we wish for this land all the advancement that civilization can bring, still we would stay the hand of progress and preserve yet many years Mexico's pristine characteristics that make it so quaint, so strange, so fascinating!

We made our first stop at the adobe village of Santa Anita, which, with the exception of a schoolhouse and church, is unchanged since the time of Cortez. The whole appearance was very strange, unlike any Indian town we had yet seen. Here we took another boat and were poled about awhile among the famous "chinampas," or floating gardens, our Indian stopping at some of them and picking flowers for us until we had all our hands could hold.

These gardens — one of the wonders of Aztec civilization — were constructed by the Aztecs in their poverty of land, and were made as follows: They bound together reeds, rushes, and bushes into a raft, and on this placed sediment from the bottom of the lake, and strips of turf, until gradually an island was formed three hundred or four hundred feet long and three or four feet deep. Sometimes willow poles were driven through the islands into the ground, and these poles, taking root, helped to hold the land more securely. In the process of time many of these islands have become solid, as were these at Santa Anita, but farther up the lakes are others, more recently formed, that properly deserve the term "floating."

It is said that criminals have sometimes escaped their pursuers by diving under these islands.

There were never more ideal gardens than these; for, with a rich soil, a hot sun above, and plenty of water at the very roots of the plants, all the requirements for a luxuriant growth are fulfilled. They are certainly a beautiful sight, and we could appreciate the feeling of the conquerors when they first beheld these "wandering islands of verdure"—a scene so new and wonderful that it seemed like "enchantment."

Leaving Santa Anita we went on a little farther amidst the same scenes, and stopped for breakfast at a queer old town where there was an inn, or "posada," with summer-houses, a garden of beautiful flowers, and a hall for dancing, sometimes used by parties coming out from the city. We thought, to make the day complete, we really ought to eat an Indian breakfast; besides, we wanted to show our friends how we fared in Guatemala; so, scorning beefsteak and other civilized dishes which the landlord offered, we ordered frijoles, tortillas, fried eggs, and coffee. As our friends tasted their breakfast rather carefully and reluctantly, we said, "How would you like this fare for ten days?"

and then, if not before, we appeared in their eyes in something the character of heroes.

At this point we had to decide the question whether we should go on toward the lakes or return to the city, and began to interview our boatman on the subject, the conversation with him being one of those amusing experiences of which we had so many. He talked Spanish so fast and so indistinctly, that it took the combined efforts of two of us to get his meaning, and the debate was a long and earnest one. Finally, ascertaining that it was so far to the lakes that we should have to remain all night in an Indian village (a far less desirable place in Mexico than Guatemala), we decided to return to the city and finish the excursion at another time.

The crowning glory of all our journey was our visit to Chapultepec, that famous castle built by the Spaniards on the site of the palace of Montezuma. The castle is reached by one of the finest boulevards in the world — the "Paseo de la Reforma" — about two miles in length, a broad, straight, smooth drive, bounded on both sides by fine avenues of trees, and adorned with beautiful statuary: the first, a fine equestrian statue of

Charles IV. of Spain, the first bronze ever cast in this hemisphere; the second, a monument to Columbus, consisting of five figures, the largest and upper being the great discover, and the others the principal Spanish missionaries; and the third, a statue not yet completed, in honor of "Guatimozin," the last of the Aztec emperors.

Every moment of the drive was a perfect delight. At the end of the boulevard, the carriage wound around the steep hill to the top, where stands the castle. The hill is of porphyry, and has a grove of cypress trees hung with festoons of Spanish moss. These cypresses are remarkable for their beauty and size, being over a hundred feet in height, and fifty feet in cirumference.

The place is by nature a strong fortification, and it was the last defence to be taken in Scott's campaign against Mexico. As we looked down upon the steep, rocky hillside, we wondered how the American army ever scaled that height as they did under fire. Just below, in the grove, is a beautiful monument to the Mexican cadets who fell in this battle, and back of the castle can be seen the battle-field of "Molino del Rey," where a skirmish occurred before the storming of Chapultepec.

The castle was built at the close of the seventeenth century, and has been the favorite residence of the Spanish viceroys, of Maximilian, and of the Mexican presidents, and it was then being repaired and remodelled for President Diaz. The military school is here, and the place is often called the "West Point" of Mexico. One of our party remarked, "If this is not a 'castle in Spain' it is the next thing to it, a Spanish castle"; and we thought of George William Curtis' delightful chapter, entitled "My Châteaux," and of all the airy structures his characters built, and felt if they could be there with us they would surely say they had at last seen something quite as fair as their own "castles in Spain."

We entered the building and wandered through the spacious rooms, broad balconies and gardens, having at every point a view of transcendent beauty — a view which we believe is unsurpassed by any in the world. Our friends, just from a seven months' tour in Europe, declared they had never seen anything more beautiful than this, — the peaceful valley of Mexico, green and smiling under a summer sky, waving with yellow corn and tropical trees, and dotted with Indian villages.

In the near distance was the great capital, with its white domes and towers; farther away were the blue lakes of Chalco and Tecuzco; and surrounding the whole valley was the great chain of mountains, among which rise the two majestic snow-crowned volcanoes of " Popocatapetl " and " Ixtaccihuatl."

Of this view a fine description is given by Prescott, as the Spaniards first beheld it from the summit of a mountain, after a toilsome march: "The valley of Mexico, with its picturesque assemblage of water, woodland, and cultivated plains, its shining cities and shadowing hills, was spread out like some gay and gorgeous panorama before them. In the highly rarefied atmosphere of these upper regions even remote objects have a brilliancy of coloring and a distinctness of outline which seems to annihilate distance. Stretching far away at their feet were seen noble forests of oak, sycamore, and cedar, and beyond, yellow fields of maize and towering maguey, intermingled with orchards and blooming gardens. In the centre of the great basin were beheld the lakes, occupying then a much larger portion than at present; their borders were thickly studded with towns and hamlets, and in the midst the fair City of Mexico, the far-famed Venice of the Aztecs. High over all rose the royal hill of Chapultepec, crowned with the same grove of gigantic cypresses which at this day fling their broad shadows over the land, and still farther on the dark belt of porphyry, girding the valley around like a rich setting, which nature had devised for the fairest of her jewels."

In the course of time, with the recession and evaporation of the lakes, the landscape has lost some of its original beauty, but even now "no traveller, however cold, can gaze on it with any other emotions than those of astonishment and rapture."

One of the most striking characteristics of the scene is the quiet serenity pervading the whole. Spenser might well have chosen it for his Palace of Morpheus, for:—

> "No noyse nor peoples troublous cryes,
> As still are won't t' anoy the walled towne,
> Might there be heard; but careles Quiet lyes,
> Wrapt in eternal silence, farre from enimyes."

It would remind one, too, of the "Happy Valley of Rasselas," which the prince and princess left to wander about the world in vain search for happiness, to return at last to their own valley again, convinced that nowhere else was happiness to be found.

Hardly a spot in the world, save the Alhambra itself, could be more fraught with romantic associations, or could stir more the sentiments and imagination. "What a place for love's young dream!" even our practical party could not help exclaiming, and felt that to make the scene complete we should have brought with us the fair Bertha and the young doctor, two of our fellow-travellers and hotel companions, who were carrying on a love affair, as we supposed, although it afterward proved a very harmless flirtation. But indulgence in revery and sentimentality was not long continued, for two of the party, on thrift intent, remembered that the carriage was waiting, and called out, "Come, we can't pay fifty cents an hour for any more romancing."

CHAPTER XXII.

HOMEWARD BOUND.

BESIDES the places of interest already described, there are many more both in and about the capital, and one could easily spend a month in constant sight-seeing with both pleasure and profit; for wherever one turns he can find something new and strange, something which makes him wish to linger, and which, when he has left, he longs to see again. The very air seems teeming with antiquity. It is never crisp and fresh as in a bright autumnal day in New England, and seems to say, "I was here years ago when the red man alone dwelt in this valley; I vibrated to the thunderings of the mighty arms of Cortez and his avaricious host, and echoed their shouts of victory; I have brooded over all the uprisings and strifes of tumultuous Mexico, and now envelop it in peace as it looks forward to advancement and a higher civilization."

Still, although there was much that tempted us to linger, longings for home and friends from whom we had been so long parted were each day becoming stronger and stronger, and almost as suddenly as we left Vera Cruz we decided to leave the City of Mexico. Accordingly, one Thursday evening we said good-bye to our friends, who were to remain a little longer, and left the city at eight o'clock by the Mexican Central Railroad. That first night we were passing through one of the dangerous portions of Mexico; the train went very slowly, and a constant watch was kept for obstructions on the track. We were told that a night rarely passed that the engineer was not obliged to stop and roll off the track great stones or other obstacles placed there for the destruction of the train. Still, as yet, there has not been a single accident on this road.

The next day we were travelling on broad tablelands, through extensive "haciendas," and strange Mexican cities. There is probably no place in the world where stock-raising is conducted on a grander scale than on these plains. One ranch sometimes covers hundreds of square miles, and possesses ten and even a hundred thousand head of cattle. Such vast estates, of course, can only be surveyed on horseback. The Mexican herdsmen pass about half their time in the saddle, are the boldest horsemen in the world, and the most expert in the use of the lasso.

At every station were the same curious, interesting scenes we have already described, venders and beggars being as numerous as ever. The device my father employed to get rid of them, and also to take a little revenge, was to answer "mañana" to all their entreaties. This made some of them indignant, although not a few appreciated the joke, for these people are often remarkably quick.

There is not the same display of military force on this road as on that from Vera Cruz, but at all the stations greatest care has to be exercised against thieves. Everything that it is possible for a man to lift has to be taken in at night and locked up. Before this was done, the people stole even the car-couplings. When the train stops for meals, either the conductor or porter has to stay in the car and keep watch, or lock all the doors, otherwise these Mexicans would enter and steal everything they could put their hands on, even to the brushes and towels in the toilet-room.

We took dinner at "Aguas Calientes," so called from the hot springs found there. It is one of the prettiest cities in Mexico, with wide streets, and handsome plazas, and has a population of about forty thousand.

That evening we reached Zacatecas, the centre of one of the great mining districts of Mexico. The grade is quite steep here, and from a ridge called the "Bufa," a fine view is had of this, one of the quaintest towns of Mexico, of the surrounding hills containing rich mines, and of the far-stretching plains below. In this city street cars are run in rather a novel fashion. Six mules are required to draw the cars to the top of the hill on which the city is situated, but at the top the mules are taken off and the car, full of passengers, is let loose to run down the hill by the force of gravitation. It must indeed be rather exciting to run down the steep hill in a horse-car at this rapid rate.

The next morning dawned upon a desolate country, and all Saturday we travelled through what was little better than a desert, — a hot, dusty plain covered with sage, buffalo grass, and thorny cactus, with only rugged, dreary mountains visible in the distance. Occasionally we passed a stream or river where trees and a little grass made a veritable oasis in the desert. There were few people living in these dreary wastes, and we wondered that there were any. They of course lived in a wretched way, in hovels and dug-outs, with little to eat except the fruit of the cactus. The desolation of the country had been increasing since we left Mexico. The change even from the day before was great, and was strikingly shown in the simple fact that the price of oranges had advanced from one cent to five cents apiece. Of course, all provisions have to be brought here by the train, and the restaurants in which we had our meals were as unique as original,— old baggage-cars by the side of the track, into which we climbed by some wooden steps.

In our Pullman, the passengers were nearly all Americans, and we became as well acquainted as if on board a steamer. We especially enjoyed conversation with a Congressman from Vermont, and with a gentleman of Cuban family.

Sunday morning we arrived in Paso del Norte, the last station in Mexico, where we received a visit from the custom-house officers, of whose strictness we had heard appalling stories, and we had to pay our first and only duty in the journey, — a duty on Mexican "curios," not, however, an exorbitant one. Leaving this station we crossed the Rio Grande and were at El Paso, Tex., where we were for the first time in many months under our own stars and stripes. We had left behind us the "land of the Montezumas," — that land of "sunny climes," of grand scenery, and of wondrous ruins; we had left behind a people as unlike ourselves as is their country; a people just waking up from their dream of the past to take their place in the progress of to-day; and we had left behind, too, their language, which, with all the rest and perhaps more than all the rest, had charmed us.

Right here we must speak a word for the Spanish language, which is not properly appreciated. It has not yet been adopted in schools, and recognized among students, as it seems to us it should be, on an equality with French and German; but a movement has already started in this direction; and now that there is such an outlook for increased commercial relations between the United States and Spanish-speaking countries, particularly Mexico, it will doubtless soon take its place as a study quite as useful and far more pleasing, as we believe, than the other two.

Its importance and the extent to which it is spoken are by no means fully realized. It is generally thought of as confined to the small and not very powerful kingdom of Spain, while in reality its territory is one of the most extensive in the world, embracing, besides Spain, Mexico, Central and South America, the West Indies, the Canary and Philippine Islands, and parts of Africa. On this side of the Atlantic alone it is spoken by sixty millions of people, so that here on our own continent English is really in the minority!

Spanish, as is well known, is an offspring from the Latin. When the rude barbarians of the North came down in such hordes upon Southern Europe and conquered the Roman Empire, their language, the Gothic, mingled with the Latin, and in time produced the "Romance Languages," — French, Spanish, and Italian. The principal changes the Latin underwent were a general softening, and a loss in declension, for the complicated system of the Latin was too much for the rude Northern tribes to master; and doubtless children of the present generation, first grappling with the Latin grammar, would gladly follow their example if they could. From its kinship to the Latin and French, a knowledge of these two languages is a great help in learning Spanish, which is generally considered a very easy language to acquire, as indeed it is, although there is a vast difference between a thorough and a superficial knowledge. It is very easy, especially with a knowledge of Latin and French, to learn to read Spanish, and to speak all that is required to express the ordinary wants of everyday life, such as a traveller would need in making a journey in Mexico, the West Indies, or Spain; but it is no easy or insignificant task to thoroughly master the language, and even the most scholarly will find sufficient intellectual gymnastics in the study.

During our journey we heard various languages, but none were so pleasing as this. There is something about the sound of it and the manner in which the people speak it, that is perfectly captivating, and makes everybody that hears it wish to speak it too. Its musical character is well known and generally recognized. It can, however, sound very disagreeable, if uttered by a rude person, with a harsh voice; and in some parts of Guatemala, as used by the country women, it was no more pleasing than the quacking of ducks, which it very much resembled. But when spoken by a cultured person it is to our ears as sweet as any music in the world. George Eliot speaks thus of it:—

> The talk of Spanish men
> With Southern intonation, vowels turned
> Caressingly between the consonants,
> Persuasive, willing, with such intervals
> As music borrows from the wooing birds,
> That plead with subtly curving, sweet descent.

There is none sweeter save the Italian, and what that gains in this respect it loses in strength, in which the Spanish is by no means wanting. From the Arabic during the eight hundred years of the Moorish rule in Spain, it acquired vigor and richness and that oriental coloring which distinguishes it among the other Romance languages. It possesses, also, a majesty which makes it well fitted to express dignity and pathos, and it is very poetic, far more so than the English. This characteristic we often noticed even in our guides, who, from the common people as they were, frequently surprised us with the poetic manner in which they expressed very ordinary and commonplace thoughts. Brevity and conciseness are also characteristic, for the Spanish often expresses in two words what the English can only say in four or five, and this conciseness of course renders it the more forcible and pithy. Spanish proverbs are noted above all others for their sharpness, deep thought, and wit.

Its great wealth of polite phrases has already been mentioned. These are often of a most extravagant nature, but the majority of the forms of courtesy and salutation are very pleasing, and supply a lack which exists in our own language. It is also very rich in augmentatives and diminutives, which are both pretty and expressive, and by these and other properties the language is rendered capable of expressing finer shades of meaning than the English.

Every language, like every nation, has its own part to perform and its own peculiar characteristics. The Spanish language seems especially adapted to express the tenderest relations of life, and the strongest and most exalted emotions of mankind — as love, affection, devotion, patriotism, reverence, and even religious worship. As bearing on this point, and showing this characteristic of the language, we would mention a teacher of languages who often speaks Spanish with his wife, preferring it to his own language (French) or to hers (English). It is well known that it is a most unusual and remarkable thing for a Frenchman to praise any language save his own, much more to prefer any other to his own, yet we met in our travels a most highly cultivated French lady who also expressed this preference, and we felt there was no higher compliment possible for the Spanish. As illustrating the especial office of Spanish, we would also refer to a great linguist who, it is said, spoke "German to his horses, French to his valet, Italian to his mistress, and Spanish to his family," and to an eminent elocutionist who said, "English is the language for business, French for conversation, Italian for love-making, and Spanish for God."

Spanish countries, the Spanish people, and the Spanish language certainly have a fascination for Americans. It may be because of the diametrically opposite characteristics; for one is an affectionate, demonstrative, exceedingly polite, slow, and improvident race, while the other is in comparison a cold, undemonstrative, brusque, nervous, and energetic race. There is something about these countries, when you have once visited them, that makes you long to go again. Every one of our party in Mexico began to talk about going to Spain the next year, and even now with any thought of a journey first comes to our minds Spain, or the West Indies, or Mexico, and we verily believe they have, in one sense, more attractions than all the glories of Europe. Bayard Taylor, the great traveller, expressed this sentiment in writing of his travels in Spain. He says, "In fact, although I have seen little fine scenery since leaving Seville, have had the worst of weather, and no very pleasant travelling experiences, the country has exercised a fascination over me which I do not quite understand. I feel myself constantly on the point of making a vow to return again."

But to continue our homeward journey. At El Paso the Mexican Central ends, and we changed to the Atchison, Topeka & Santa Fé Railroad. Having to wait two hours for the train, we had time to walk about and see the town, which is merely a railroad centre, the meeting-place of five different railroads.

The railroad crosses a corner of Texas and then enters New Mexico, which it traverses from south to north. This territory, once belonging to Mexico, bears marks of it still in adobe villages, in quite a percentage of Mexican inhabitants, and in its quaint capital, Santa Fé, the oldest town in North America. The whole territory is a grazing country and has a barren look, although not as desolate as that through which we travelled the day before. Steele says of it: "Burro trains, adobe castles, higgledy-piggledy villages are everywhere. Sunshine of the yellowest variety seems to shine always. It is a world of black lava blocks, gaunt cacti, frowning ranges of sierras, and profound and unbroken peace. There are sometimes running streams that seem to have been mysteriously coaxed uphill, and gardens whose green luxuriance surprises the eye."

The next morning we arrived at the station of Las Vegas. Six miles from here are the hot springs, a charming watering-place and health resort. We had made our plans to stop here and rest, as it had been recommended as a place well worth visiting; but when we reached here all the tempting pictures and descriptions displayed in our books and railway guides could not induce us to stop, so anxious were we to press on toward home. It only seemed as if the train would not go fast enough.

Leaving New Mexico we passed through the southeast corner of Colorado, in sight of the Spanish Peaks, and then crossed the state line into Kansas. One of the passengers pointed out to us the old Santa Fé trail and the rambling house of Kit Carson, in a lonely region. Near this spot the train passes through quite a remarkable tunnel, and we went forward to get the full benefit of the scene. The road at this point is built on the hillside and has quite a grade.

We traversed Kansas from west to east, — a flourishing state, with rich soil and fine climate, growing cities, and a progressive population. Between six and seven o'clock that evening (Tuesday) we arrived at Kansas City, and were so tired with five days' continuous travelling that we concluded to stop for rest and refreshment. This is a great railroad and business centre, one of those western cities which have sprung up like mushrooms in a night and attained marvellous growth.

The next day we left at evening by the Chicago,

Rock Island & Pacific, crossing Missouri and Illinois, and arriving in Chicago the next afternoon, where we stopped, and were entertained by the representative of the firm. His was the first familiar face we had seen since we left home, and if he ever meets anybody more delighted to see him he may count himself a happy man; for how welcome a sight a familiar face was, only those can appreciate who have had a like experience. He showed us all about the city, which we had not visited since the fire, and we noted great changes. We had also the pleasure of meeting the rest of the family of our travelling companions in Mexico.

But we could not linger long even in so attractive a city as Chicago; our great wish was now to reach home as soon as possible, and we began to look up the various routes to Boston. Almost every state after entering the United States had in it some acquaintance or some college friend which tempted us to stop; and now especially were there friends by the way, but still greater than all other desires was that to reach home. It was Friday, and we thought of the Sunday which was soon to come, when all the family would be at home longing for us even as we longed for them; we thought what a pleasant day it would be to spend together, and how dreary if apart, and thereupon decided we must take the route which would bring us home Sunday morning. Accordingly we left Chicago that night by the Michigan Central. At Niagara the train stopped long enough to give us a fine view of the Falls. Saturday we were in the southern part of Canada, and "winter, lingering in the lap of spring," treated us to a snow-storm, as if to defy our attempt to escape his reign. What a change had come over the scene since the beginning of our railway journey, and how far the "iron horse" had brought us, even from the glory and sunshine of the tropics to the cold storms of winter!

In the morning we were once more in dear old Boston, and joyfully greeted by the friends who sadly parted with us so many weeks before. What joy there was that day in many hearts we shall not undertake to tell!

Very few, perhaps none, save ourselves, who took this journey, can ever know the whole. Much pleasure there was, to be sure, but more pain; much to enjoy, but far more to endure. Without an aim, a definite purpose, it could never have been accomplished. One went with all the ardor and zeal of an explorer; the other, at first, chiefly with the thought of pleasure, but, as it proved in reality, to help, sustain, and care for her leader.

Our sojourn in Mexico and Guatemala City was a real pleasure, but what enjoyment we derived from the rest is much to our own credit. We think even Mark Tapley, if he had been with us, would have felt he had at last found places where there was real "credit in being jolly." Begging the liberty to speak a word for ourselves, we will say that hearts less brave, courage less persistent, judgment less sound to plan, and will less strong to execute, would have fainted and fallen by the way before the journey was half completed. Neither would we fail gratefully to acknowledge the divine Providence who as truly led and kept us as He did the children of Israel in their wanderings.

www.ingramcontent.com/pod-product-compliance
Lightning Source LLC
Chambersburg PA
CBHW030744230426
43667CB00007B/837